Mystic Saints Of India:1

Shankaracharya

B. K. CHATURVEDI

Series Editor : Dr. Mahendra

BOOKS FOR ALL
Delhi-110052

Distributed by :
D. K. Publishers Distributors Pvt. Ltd.
1, Ansari Road,
New Delhi-110 002
Phs. : 327 8368, 326 1465
Fax : 326 4368
E-mail : dkpd@del3.vsnl.net.in
Web site:www.dkpd.com.

First Published : 2000

ISBN 81-7386-222-2 (Shankaracharya)
ISBN 81-7386-231-1 (Series)

Published by :
Books For All
B-2, Vardhaman Palace,
Nimri Commercial Centre,
Near Ashok Vihar Phase-IV,
Delhi-110 052
Ph. : 740 1672, 745 2453
E-mail : lpp@nde.vsnl.net.in
Web site:www.lppindia.com.

Printed at :
D. K. Fine Art Press Pvt. Ltd.
Delhi-110052 Ph. 745 2451

Printed in India

CONTENTS

BOOK II

Shankaracharya's Selected Works

(Their Original Text, Romanised Version Along With Hindi & English Translation)

Introduction

The contribution of the mystic saints in consolidating and rejuvenating the perennial Indian thought and in shaping the Indian ethos has never been fulhy assessed for the benefit of our awakened but not learned readership. It is with this intention the present series of books has the planned and this book is the first flower of that mystic garden.

Indubitably, Shankarachanya stands as the colossus among the Indian saints of comparatively recent origin - distinct from the Rishi-Muni tradition of yore- who moulded the indigenous thought with his brilliant expositons of the sacred texts. But his philosophical interpretations of the sacred text was not only an exercise in intellectual gymnastics but it also had it ethical and sociological impact. Although his achivements have been much wide and varied, the attempt through this work has been to show their representative glimpses to our curious readers. It is for this purpose that his selected works havealso been translated in Hindi and English to help them get a 'feel' of the original. His terse philosophical interpretations of the sacred texts have been also explained in a lucid and easy to comprehend language with a liberal dose of examples from the contemporary life. It is hoped that to our 'root-finding generation' this look will be an asset.

Lastly, the author expresses his gratitude to Mittal Brothers of 'Books for All' for giving him an opportunity to write this Book.

- B.K. Chaturvedi

Series' Editor's Notes

In 1963, Dr. Radhakrishan, the President of India, declared in Bombay, "The time has come for all countries to work towards making the world a single home for Humanity....Economics, politics and transport have done their jobs. What we have to do is to give a soul to the world which has found a body. You can give it if you are truly Indian." We Indians are proud to have so many mystic saints in our history who can contribute to the upliftment of the human being.

In Infdian thinking, there are two modes in which we acquire knowledge : Argument and Experiment. Both these modes, together with experience play an important role in the development of Mankind. Saints of India, through their arguments, tried to communicate their experiences to human beings. They represent an advanture in thinking.

This series, it is hoped, will enable the reader, eastern or western, to understand and appreciate currents of Indian thoughts By depicting the life and writings of different saints, we have tried to portray the true picture of Indian culture. I am really thankful to all those, who have elped in preparing and publishin these books, as it will not only propagate the ideas of Indian saints, but also help in making the mankind a better race.

Our world, becomes wider, our imagination richer and our life more colourful and more gestful as the result of our companion ship with these saints, who are the travellers of the spirit and the pioneers of thought.

25.7.1999 **Dr. Mahendra**

Book 1

1. Shankaracharya : The Thinker and Guru Par Excellence

Indeed Shankaracharya in the brightest beacom among the revered saints of India. But he is not the thinker like thinkers are normally reckoned to be, for he is many persons rolled into one personality. He is a thinker, incomparable metaphysicist, seer, saviour of the Santan Dharma, a statesman having clear vision of India's unity, a social reformer and a brilliant poet. He had achieved in his only thirty two years what a whole race might not achieved in three centuries. F.W.F. Tomlin writes : "his incesssant labours in the service of the orthodox human faith had rendered him not an old man before his time-because he seems always to have been adult -but a man for whom half a life time had consumed energies normally expended in half a dozen.' Observing in the same vein, Sister Nivedita (Miss Margaret Noble)' says "Western people can hardly imagine a personality like that of Shankaracharya. We contemplate with wonder and delight the devotion of Francis of Assisi, the intellect of Abelard, the virile force and freedom of Martin Luther and the political efficiency of Ignatius Loyola. But who can imagine all these united in one person."

Indeed he was a human being with the divine spark. What normal human being would have achieved in ten lives he had accomplished not only in one life hut in the half span of the normal human age. That his thinking been still astounds modern scholars is still a great proof of his erudition and originality. We shall be discussing his these qualities later on hut suffice it to say that the school of philosophy established by him is still venerated by most logical thinkers of the modern era.

What has been scantily paid attention to is the organising capabilities of Adi Shankarachara. He lived in an age which can he called dark age for the Hinduism. It was an age of disorder and decay with the Sanatan Dharm, as the way of Hindu life is normally called, taking beating from every side. While inherent contradictions not removed for centuries had made it hollow from inside, the rise of the Buddhism had also dealt upon it a telling blow. Obviously when your ranks are divided and rows daggers drawn with each other, any outsider is powerful enough to take up your citadel. Shankarachaya not only repaired the form of the Hinduism not also revived its basic spirit. In fact what the Hinduism was suffering from before the advent of Shankarchaya was total insulation between the spirit and form. Those who pursued its spirit only became totally cut off with the then society because they were unable to explain the importance of the spirit though they were very much realising it themselves. On the other hand those who confined their adherence to Hinduism to performing only the rituals like Havans, ostentatious form of worshipping various gods by almost humanising the deities etc, didn't feel the need of knowing as to why were they performing the action so ignorantly. And this communicaton gap between the two basic links of the faith they owed allegiance to was yawing day by day. While one had the body, the other had the spirit. The spirit becomes an eerie existence like a ghost with out the body while the body becomes dead when devoid of the spirit or the soul. It was at this juncture that Shankarachaya or Shankar as he is commonly called - emerged to form the bridge; to corelate the two sectors of the Hindu, nay Indian society, about nearly one and quarter millennia back. He as well fortified the spirit as he rejuvenated the body. Not only he wrote many commentaries on the Vedic text to explain the real meaning that they enshrined but he also told the Karmakandis (ritualists) how to perform and why to perform a particular worship. He created the four famous 'Maths' (seat of religious authority) across the length and the breath of the country with clear indication that who would perform worship where among these four citadels Hinduism.

It won't be incongruous to throw some light on his concept of national (which may be loosely interpreted as the whole expanse of religion) unity and his devising methods to make this faith service itself through mutual consulltation After having built four religious seat of authority at Joshimath near Badrimath (U.P) Sharada math at Dwarikapuri (Gujarat), Govard hanamath at Jagannathpuri (Puri) in Orissa and Shringerimath in Mysore (Karnatka) he not only ordained in which region which Gotra's Brahman would be head-priest at which peetha, he also devised a novel means of ensuring their interaction after a gap of fixed period. It is believed that its was he who started (or revived) the Kumbh-Mela festival after a gap of an astrological unit of time, i.e. twelve years or so. Many people might not be aware of this fact hence it needs a little elaboration.

Notwithstanding the mythological story of Churning the Ocean to procure nectar, the fact is that it is not known when the Kumbh Mela in the present form was started and who was the real founder or the first organiser of this fair.

There is no mention about it in the published Puranas about "Kumbhasnana yoga". No reference has so far been traced from any inscriptions or from writings of early periods about the holding of kumbh Mela. The Chinese pilgrim Hieun-tsang, when visited and stayed in India from 629 A.D to 695 A.D and is well known for giving copious details of what he heard and saw, stayed at Prayag for some time during the reign of Harsharvardhan (606-647 AD) and he has not mentioned anything about the practice of holding Kumbha Mela at this place. He, however, makes a reference regarding somewhat similar large gathering of people at Prayag during Harsha's reign. This king, Harshavardhan, used to arrange every five years at that place a huge assembly of priests, monks and ascetics and of people of all religions faiths and beliefs, and of chieftain and elites, and of common peoples, who totalled half a million or so. It was arranged with the apparent aim to facilitate intermixing of the people all strata, to bring about a synthesis of different schools of thought and cultures, to foster tolerance for all faith and religions and create in them a sort of solidarity. There is, however no record of this practice continuing after the death of king Harshavardhana. It is generally believed that it was Adi Sharkarachanya or the first Sharkarachanya who revived the tradition linking it with the astrological singularness of the planets. He revived the tradition and stimulated the idea of an assembly of saints and monks different sects and belief of Hindu faith from all parts of India, at different places at some internal, to strengthen the unity of our wide-based Hindu faith and culture. It was also to consolidate this faith in the entire Aryavarta (old name of the undivided India) that he chose the four citadels of religious authority. Shankarachanya in his very young age seemed to have realised that any faith would decay if not regularly rejuvenated by joint efforts since it is like a stream that flows on the right course when it has dams and bridges built at the right position. He knew that Hinduism, in- herently, is a very catholic and all-pervasive yet strong faith always retaining its identity like the pious Ganga river but it has to be cleansed occasionally and its basic truths need to be logically intrepreted in every age. It is only when it lacked these rejuvenating measures that it lost its dynamism and became unreliable to be 'outsmarted' by other faiths.

In this light Shankaracharya appears to be the Saviour of Sanatan Dharma and shows his extra ordinary capabilities as an administrator and organiser. And all these feats he had achieved with in three decades or so. For we know that his mortal age terminated at 32 Getting born in far-off South in Kerela, writing all these commentaries on the Vedic text, and hymns for various deities, organising worship, convincing the gullible to come back to the Sanatan Dharm Fold, reviving the old traditions of holding huge fairs like the Kumbha Mela etc - all these major achievements were accomplished in such a short period

Apart from doing all this he also enunciated the theory of Advaitwad. Even if we discard Shankar's miracles as legend and tradition, it detracts no whit from his greatness, not because of these but because of his peerless philosophy he gave to the world. The Advait Vedanta of Shankar is probably one of the very few creeds which rests on no dogma since unlike most other schools of Hinduism it believes uncompromisingly in a formless god which gives it at once an international status. Secondly it makes pure knowledge its base. Also, with its concept of 'Moksha' it provides a positive solution to the endless chains of births and deaths. It should be understood that Shankarachaya's enunciation is not for the sake of intellectual gymnastics but goes to the every core of life's ills since it tackles the problem of suffering in a novel and effective manner. More of it shall be discussed when we mention about his theories and interpretation in a separate chapter ahead. Suffice it to say at this stage that Shankaracharya showed to humanity a practical way of getting beyond the miseries that life entails.

Shankarchanya's all there achievements had made Charles Jhonston say: What shall we say, then, of the Master Shankar ? Is he not the guardian of the sacred waters, who by his commentaries had hemmed about, against all impurities or Time's jealousy, first the mountain tarn of the Upamishads then the serene Lake of the Srimadbhagwat Gita, and last the deep reservoir of the Sutra, adding from the generous riches of his wisdom, lovely fountains and lakelats of his own, the crest Jewel, the Awakening the Discernment ?"

But how did he achieve all this ? What was his background, where was he born, who was his guru - all these questions have been auswered in the coming pages.

2. His Early life

Believed to be an incarnation of lord Shankar, although his family's chosen deity was Lord Krishna, Shankaracharya was born in Kaladi, a quiet village on the bank of the river Churna or Purna about one km.. from the town Alwaye, on the fifth day of the bright half of the lunar month Vaishakh (15th April to 15th May) under the constellation of Punarvasu in 788 A.D. His father's name was Shivguru and his mother Aryamba. This pious couple of the Namboodari caste represented all this is believed to be best in this high caste Brahmin Gotra. The Namboodari Brahmins of Kerala are highly cultured and deeply religious people. Shivguru and his wife were learned, virtuous, wealthy, large hearted and liberal. They had every thing that a noble couple of that era could aspire for except that they didn't have a son. On the advise of a roving mendicant they decided to go to the nearby shrine of Shivakshetra (Trichur) and pray to god for a male child. Observing strict vows they continued to stay there, bathing daily in the sacred river, visiting the temple and worshipping Lord Shiv. At last the lord was pleased with this piety and appearing to them in the from of Brahmin[1] asked th e couple as to what his desire was. Overjoyed with their prayer being answered, Shivguru revealed his desire of getting a son. "You can have several sons of long and fully mature age but dull of wit as also a very brilliant and enlightened son but of short age. Make your choice," It was difficult matter to decide : dull witted sons of long age and an enlightened one of shortage.[2] So they left the choice with the Lord Himself. That Brahman gave the hint that Lord Shiv himself be born as their son and advised them to return to their home in Kaladi"

Shivaguru and Aryamba returned home delighted. Happily they distributed charity to the poor and inviting noble saints and pious seers at their place, they fed them lovingly and offered them many gifts in anticipation of their desire's fulfilment. As Aryamba became pregnant a divine glow seemed to permeate in their enter home. And then on due day Aryamba delivered the son on the fifth day of the bright half of Vaishakh in 788 A.D.[3]

---

1. Some accounts say the Lord had appeared in Aryamba's dream.

2. Many accounts aver that the couple had chosen for a short-lived, brillint son but the latter events prove that at least the mother had no idea.

3. Although there is controversy about Shankar's year of birth, we have taken the generally accepted year.

That Shankar was prodigious child is proved by many anecdotes : The 'Madhaviya Shankaravijaya claims that : "in his first year he learnt the Sanskrit alphabet; when he was two he could read books in his mother tongue and at three he could understand the Kavyas and Puranas. Though this might appear a bit exaggerated description, we may deem it that he had developed ability to learn and understand Sanskrit before he was five. His mother, Aryamba, seeing her son's such fast development decided to hold his Upanayan Sanskar (Sacred Thread ceremony) so that he could be formally admitted to a school or sent for regular education. But, unfortunately, before that pious ceremony could take place Shivaguru died. Shankar was mature enough to console his widowed mother. Now for mother he was the only hope. After the expiry of the period of sorrow, the Upanayas Sanskar was performed. And then he was sent to a 'Gurukula' (formal school) for the study of the Vedas and other branches of knowledge. But surprisingly, what a normal student could achieve in thirty years,, Shankar accomplished in just two years. In this brief time he achieved mastery over the Scriptural text (Dharmashashtra, Puranas and Upanishad) Nyaya (jurisprudence)] Sankhya Yoga (mathematics and logic), Itihas and other branches of knowledge, taught then. As was compulsory for the students, he lived by begging alone. It was in one of his sojourns for getting food that an unusual event took place.

One day when the boy was Shankar going about begging for the alms as was the custom, he happened to visit the house of a Brahmin woman. She was extremely poor herself and didn't have even a grain of rice to offer as alms to the begging student. At last with great difficulty she could find a stale myrobalam fruit (Anwala) which she very diffidently dropped into the begging bowl of the boy. She felt very much embarrassed hut she had no choice. Shankar devined her devotion and was overwhelmed with pity for the poverty of that Brahmin family. While moving away he uttered a sincere prayer to Lakshmi, the goddess of riches, imploring her to bless the woman with wealth. His this prayer is known as the famous Kanakadhara - Strotra (Prayer for the Shower of gold) which is believed to be Shankar's earliest compositons. And lo and behold ! his prayer to Lakshmi was answered immediately. The goddess did shower 'Amalakas' (anwalas) of gold inside the house, much to the joy and amazement of the poor Brahmin family. The couple prostrated themselves before the divine child and worshipped him. This was a miracle the boy Shankar had performed for the sake of that poor Brahmin lady.

In fact all such miracles-as they are called - were performed by Shankar for giving relief to others and not for his own personal gain. As is generally believed miracles are performed by divine persons never for any personal benefit. Many a time we think in our minds that why those who are credited with performing great miracles appear always clad in rags and they stay in small huts. If they have such powers why don't they stay in huge palace ? Why don't they themselves become prime ministers, kings and presidents by virtue of there divines powers ? Why should have Mother Teresa kept on arranging funds for her 'Missionaries of Charity if she had the divines power of having others wishes fulfilled ? In fact answer to all there question remains enshrined in the essential bed - rock of all religions: selflessness. If you have any such power it would show its efficacy in the case of the most needy one ; in amelerioalting the suffering of other and never for any person's - no matter howsoever 'great' or 'revered'- selfish ends. History bears testimony to the fact that all truly great humans had their this power rendered ineffective when used for their selfish end. It is true that Shankarchanya himself didn't belong to a very rich and affluent family but he couldn't have made the goddess of wealth, Lakshmi, pour a stream of gold-embedded 'Anwala' into his house ! There miracles get a sort of divine sanction when performed for a genuine cause. This digression has been necessitated by the desire to highlight the fact that all these great persons and incarnations grace the mortal world for furthering noble causes and not for enjoying all pleasures of life themselves.

That Shankaracharya or boy Shankar was a child prodigy has already been mentioned. His progress at the 'Gurukul' was swift and stupendous. He had acquired all the knowledge that his teachers could teach him and hence, ere-long his teacher blessed him and gave him the leave to depart. He returned home, and began to impart knowledge of what he had learnt to the students who cared to come to him. His erudition and wisdom soon became the talk of the regions, and his fame began to spread far and wide. It cven reached the ears of Rajshekhar, the then king of Kerala, who sent his minister to invite the boy to the palace. But how could one who had renounced all sense-desires seek the pleasures of the court ? The boy Shankar neither accepted the costly royal gifts bestowed on him, nor agreed to go to the king's palace. The devout and considerate king, then, him self came to Kaladi to pay his respects to the boy sage. Since king Rajshekhar was himself a poet and playwright he recited his composition to the boy sage and was delighted to hear the boys - sage's erudite comments.

It was some time after the boy sage's return to home that he wrought another miraclo. IIis mother, Aryamba used to go to the sacred river Churna (Purna) which though flowed nearly yet she had to walk for some distance, since the river was on the out - skirts of the town . One summer day when the sun was unusually scorching, she was struck by the overpowering heat and fainted on the way. When she didn't return by the usual time, Shankar was worried and went in reach of her. He was worried to see her lying unconsious. Sprinkling some water on her face he sat by her side, fanning up air frantically by a big leaf. She was soon revived and then he conducted her back home safely. Shankar was now worried for her mother. Knowing that he would not be able to dissuade her to suspend her schedules of going to the river every day, he realised that her going to the river would be hazardous for her frail body. Then, finding no solution to the problem, Shankar prayed to lord Krishna, his family deity, to make the river flow closer to his home. Night and day he besought the god, till lord Krishna was moved with his earnest prayers. That year, it is said, it rained so heavily that the river changed its course a bit and eventually started flowing very close to Aryamba's house. Inhabitants of the village who knew Aryamba's problem were amazed with the power of prayer of boy Shankar.

When Shankar was about to complete his eight years some sages happened to visit his house. They were pleased with the treatment they received and they were really delighted to know how precocious and brilliant Aryamba's only son was. The sages then disclosed to the lady that her son had come to fulfil a divine mission and although he was initially destined to live only eight years, this span would now he doubled by the divine decree. Their this prediction about her son's age reminded Aryamba of the choice that lord Shiv had placed before her and her husband when He had appeared in the form of a Brahmin in answer to her prayer. But it was only now that she realised that which of the two alter natives was chosen. Never - the less she was distraught with grief to know that her son would die early. Then the boy Shankar comforted her by impressing upon her that any association of the two souls in this mortal world is by sheer chance and always of temporary duration . "The coming together of people, "he said, was like the brief meeting of the travellers. It is a sheer coincidence described by the expression" "Nadi-naav sanjog," i.e the chance - meeting of a boat with a river."

However, rather than reconciling to the decree of destiny-as she believed the sage's foretelling to be true- Aryamba became more alarmed seeing her tender-aged son developing ascetic tendencies. She felt apprehensive lest he abandon home. In order to make him change his mind she started diverting his attention to domestic duties. She began to seek a suitable bride for him. But Shankar had no desire for such a life. He had mentally become too mature to get drawn towards these worldly pleasures although physically he was of the age when children remain engrossed in playing with toys. But he had seen that how fey were much attractions. He was firm on renouncing the world and become an ascetic. Although her mother was adamant to keep him bound by domestic duties he achieved his objective by an incident which took place quite accidentally.

Now, since the river Churna had started flowing closeby his home, one day he entered it for having his bath. His mother was also nearby. Suddenly a huge crocodile caught hold of his leg. Shankar called out to his mother : "Help ! a crocodile has caught hold of me." Aryamba immediately came closer, to the bank, overwhelmed with anxiety and fear. With other persons' help who had assembled on the bank she tried hard to have her son's leg detached from the jaws of that crocodile. But the crocodile had caught hold of his leg so firmly that even their joint efforts failed to free Shankar. Then Shankar said : "Mother ! this crocodile in pulling me away. I am about do die. You haven't permitted me to take 'Sannyasa' (renunciation from the world) without which I cannot achieve liberation. If even now you allow me to take the vow of asceticism, by the grace of Almighty, I will be able to get Moksha."[1] Seeing that her word would fulfil his son's desire - apparently, the last one - Aryamba gave her consent immediately. In fact she had no other alternative. No sooner than the permission was granted did Shankar, the boy sage, embrace sannyas. As he did so, miraculously the crocodile released him and the boy saint came out from the river unharmed. This incident marked the most significant turning point of his life. Many accounts aver that the whole plot was conceived and implemented with divine machinations at Shankar's request, for he knew that without such compulsive reasons her mother wouldn't have allowed him to embrace sannyas.

1. Sannyas literally means becoming equidistant from every live or dead object of the world. That is the primary state for attaining to the level of total disirelessness or Moksha.

Nevertheless, Aryamba was overjoyed at her son's escape from the jaws of crocodile, complacently, like a dotting mother thinking that Shankar would now settle down and get married, and the incident would be forgotten. But she had no idea how determined her son was for his implementing his vow of Sannyas. He was hardly eight, an age unconceivable for becoming a Sannyasi as even the scriptures ordain that not before 16 such a vow should he fulfilled. Inherent in this decree is the potential Sannyasi's not forsaking his initial and obligatory worldly duties. Aryamba must have thought that when the custom was on her side which deterred the only male member in the family embracing Sannyas. But Shankar was quite firm in his resolve for it was what he had been aspiring all these years and now since the biggest hurdle-mother's permission miraculously crossed he looked froward to his wandering all over the country and doing what he always wanted to do. On being asked to stay home, the young boy replied with a gleam in his eyes : "Henceforth whole world shall be my home, and all women who give me alms my mother". He who gives me instructions I will regard, as my father and who seeks wisdom for me my guru." Then he asked Aryamba to allow him to go out in search of a guru who might formally initiate him to the order of Sannyas. Seeing his mother perturbed he also promised that he would return to her whenever she needed him. He further assured her that he would be at her side when she was on her death- bed and despite his vows of ascetism, he would perform her last rites. This might appear rather an incongruous a commitment but it must be realised that during those times, particularly in traditional families, a son- that too an only one- not performing last rites of his parents was considered a grossly negligent son, callous about his sacred duty[1]. Having thus consoled and reassured her mother and having arranged with his relations for his mother's adequate maintenance and protection, Shankar took her blessings and crossed the threshold of his home to accomplish the mission he was born for. Now as a beacon lighting the entire firmament he began to move about to get from, and give knowledge of the Ultimate to, the world at large.

1. Sannyasi are normally prohibited from performing these rites since they are supposedly not obliged to perform their any worldly duties.

3. In Quest of Knowledge

Shankar, the boy was a bout eight years old when he abandoned home for the pursuit of knowledge. Though believed to be an in carnation of Lord Shiv himself he was hardly needing a guru, he chose to follow what was the standard practice of his times. While searching for a guru, he happened to meet a Brahmin who advised him to go under the shelter of Govindapada, a great ancient sage reincarnated as the seer. Shankar was told-that Govindapada was sitting in his samadhi (trance) in some cave on the bank of the Narmada river. This sage was credited with having received the knowledge of Advaita Vedanta from his perceptor Gaudapada. Shankar had heard about him and was determined to reach him.

On his way from deep south to the river Narmada while he was resting beneath a tree to escape the oppressive heat he happened to espy a tiny pool having a few froglings jumping in restlessness, apparently due to the heat. Then Shankar saw an unusual spectacle. He was astonished to see a black cobra spreading out its hood to provide shade to the troubled froglings. "The snake whom nature had meant to feed on frogs is spreading its hood to protect the baby frogs from the heat !" Believing this place to be a divine spot he mentally decided to establish a 'Math', he moved on. Near this pond there was a hillock, the sides of which had steps to climb. Shankar went up and found a lone hut in which an ascetice was sitting. An enquiry revealed it to be a hermitage of the sage Shringi. Meeting him he proceeded further to reach the bank of the river Narmada after a long and strenuous journey.

As he reached there he found a number of aged ascetice who were eagerly awaiting to receive Govindapada's blessing. They told him that they had been there a long time, and that the great sage was sitting in a cave closeby for several hundreds of years and had not yet emerged out of his samadhi. It was generally believed-that his trance would be broken at right time, so was the decree of destiny. Shankaracharya happened to arrive on that very day when the sage was to wake up from his trance. Perhaps, Govindapada too, was aware of the coming of the fittest disciple since he had known by his yogic intuition that Shankaracharya was the incarnation of lord Shiva and the god himself had sent him to get the knowledge in Advait Vedanta[1]. And as soon as Shankar stopped in the cave Govindapada saw him, and was impressed with the saintly appearance of that divine boy. He was delighted to have found in him

1. This term shall be elaborated in the coming pages.

the person he was waiting to instruct to all this while. Govindapada's own guru, the venerable Gaudapada had instructed him in the Advaita teachings as contained in the 'Brahma Sutra'. He gladly initiated the gifted boy into these truths and those contained in the Uparishads. The sage boy Shankar stayed there many days, humbly receiving the knowledge he was seeking. Then yet another miracle took place.

Those were the days when our hills were lush green with vegetation and trees were not cut so mercilessly as they are nowadays. So it rained a lot. One day it rained as much as, much as to make the mighty Narmada over-flow its banks and threaten to inundate the hill and the cave. Govindapad was sitting, lost in his samadi. His other disciples were greatly worried seeing the Narmada rise menacingly. Though they tried to put some boulders etc. on the path of the mounting sheet of water, it cound't check the ingress of the mighty Narmada. When the water was about to inundate the cave, Shankaracharya took an earthen jar and, uttering a 'mantra' over it, put it at the mouth of the cave. An soon as the flooded waters entered, they miraculously went into the earthen jar and although a regular stream poured, it was all taken by it and never had the chance to enter the cave. All the ascetics present there were amazed by this strange spectacle and they told the guru when the later came out of his trance. The sage was delighted. He had tested the devotion of Shankar and the efficacy of his disciple's mantra. Mightily impressed, he then asked Shankar to proceed further to Kashi (Vanarasi) on the next step of his initiations and pay his homage to the shrines of Vishwanth . Then he also told Shankar that the celebrated sage Vyas had foretold him "That a person who captures in a pot the nighty stream of a river was destined to write commentary on Brama-Sutra. Since you have accomplished this feat, you should now go to Kashi and achieve what you are destined for "Receiving his blessing Shankar set out to that most hellowed city for the votaries of Lord Shiv."

Reaching Kashi, Shankar took up his abode at the famous Manikarnika Ghat. Staying there he began to worship in various temples, his favourite being the shrine of Veshwanath and the temple of Annapoorna. By this time his fame had reached far and wide and a number aspirants flocked to him to be instructed in the school of Advaita Vedanta. Shankar was quite young at that time yet many aspirants vied with each other to become his disciple. His first disciple was Sadananda.

One day while Shankar was walking towards the Ganga in the company of his disciples, the group saw a 'pariah', an untouchable, coming towards him followed by four ferocious looking dogs. The pariah defiantly came in the group's way as thickly as to obstruct the total passage. Shankar asked him to get away and the pariah replied : "Who should get away from whom, O learned Brahman ? What do you want thrown out of your way : the ephemeral body or the eternal self ? The body is nourished on food and every being has its body made about of the same stuff. Since there is no difference why should one body go away from another ? And the Eternal Self is one ? How can It get away from Itself- The Indivisible Whole! Hence neither there is difference between one matter and another and one soul and another, so there is no meaning in one's going away from the other ? It is only lay people who confuse over these two; the wise alone know that spirit alone is real and not matter. He who distinguishes between a brahmin and a pariah has his wisdom deluded. Everyone is the manifestation of the same, Immutable Eternal Self. Is the sun different which shines over the holy Ganga than the sun that shines in a dirty pool ? How the high born be different from those belonging to the lowly clan ? There are verily the divisons made by the ignorant and the wise see through their inherent unity. The Self is like the calm waters of a shore loss sea, quite and undisturbed. The apparent difference is due to the adjuncts such as body which are ephemeral and illusory, of not any lasting value. So why should I be untouchable for you or anybody ?"

Shankar was amazed to hear there words loaded with Advaitic wisdom coming out of mouth of a pariah ! He mentally concluded that such wisdom could issue only from one person, the Master of Kashi, Lord Shiv. The untouchable did so with a purpose. Whatever was wanting in Shankar having been corrected, the form of an outcast pariah vanished and out emerged, Lord of Universe, the Great Vishwanath, making the four ferocious dogs also vanish, replaced by the Holy Vedas-personified! Immediately Shankar bowed before him and sang the hymn to convey his devotion and ecstasy : "from the stand-point of the body I am thine servant, part of thee; from that of soul and from the stand point of the Self, I am verily thou, for Self in One and Unique." Blessing Shankar Lord Shiv said : "Son, I am pleased with you. It is through you that I intend to disseminate Vedic teaching throughout the world. When I found you erring in recognising the reality I came in that form. Now go and start writing commentary on the Brahma Sutra. The basic theme of Advaitism is the formless supreme Spirit (or Brahm). Go and tell it every one. Let this knowledge be spread far and wide. Whatever you accomplish through your efforts-deem it an my work." Saying so, the Lord disappeared.

It was at Kashi itself where seeing an old Brahmin Chanting like a parrot the rules of Sanskrit grammar that Shankar composed his very popular hymn known as 'Bhaj govindam[1]'. Besides this he also composed his 'Dwadashmanjarikastrotra.' In fact the out burst of these verses was necessitated by his seeing the

[1] Included in the traslation section at the end of this book.

people madly devoting exclusive attention to the from rather than to the spirit. He was not against rituals and form but always emphasised on paying due attention to the spirit behind the form. His poetic brilliance had also inspired his fourtreen disciples to add to his composition, particularly to the Dwadash-manjarika-strotra hymn. It is believed that he had by this time fourteen disciples around him and each had contributed a verse.

Having received the blessings from mone other than Lord Shiv, the resolve to write his commentary on the Brahma Sutra now became quite strong in Shankaracharya's mind. He also decided that the best place to do this august work was Badrinath. Because the arch-guru, sage Vedvyas had also composed them at this place only. But it was a very difficult journey. One can imagine what would have been the situation in those days when still, despite all the modern facilities, fast vehicles and metalled road, it is considered not an easy job to reach Badrinath. Moreover, then the journey was to be almost totally under-taken on toot. Yet, undaunted, Shankaracharya set out for Badrinath, along with his disciples . Of these, Sadanand from Chola country has already been mentioned about. His other pet disciples was Prakhakar, a dweller of Shreeballipuram. His meeting his guru (Shankar) involves also an interesting story. Prabhakar had a son, 13 year old yet totally mute. In fact Prakhakar had come to Shankar to have his son treated. On Shankaracharya asking the boy who he was, the boy on his own had blurt out a series of verses in each of which he affirmed that he was the Self which is of the nature of eternal consciousness. The master was supremely pleased will that 'mute' boy and affectionately gave him the name 'Hastamalaka' which means 'one whose wisdom in as clear as a myrobalan fruit placed upon the palm of one's hand.' Leter, he was so much pleased with the boy's work that he himself wrote a commentary on it. The other disciple was one who wrote a hymn in praise of the Master in the most difficult 'Totaka' metre to earn an epithet of 'Totakacharya' from his Guru.

While going to Badrinath alongwith his disciples Shankar visited various place of pilgrimage that fell on the way. He also passed through the regions where Tantrik rites involving even human sacrifice had been quite popular apart from other base kinds of abhorsome customs. With all the authority at his command Shankarcharya persuaded the people to abandon these undesirable practices.

At last reaching Badrinath be took his shelter near the fabled shrine and began to visit the temples nearby. The pulchritude of the region was really breathtaking. There were many shrine and holy spots nearby including the famous temple of Narayan. But he was quite grieved to find that the idol of Narayan was missing from the shrine. The priest of the temple complained that the king of China had been repeatedly attacking this region with unchecked hostility as the regions had no protectors. In order to save the idol from getting defiled by the touch of a Mlechchha (vile persons of different culture) it was thought safer to throw the idol the into the famous pond called Naradakunda. Then at the behest of Shankar a search was made for the idol but in vain. At last Shankar himself decided to enter the pond although the temple priests tried to dissuade him from making the attempt as the tank was believed to be of unfathomable depth since it was said to be subterraneously connected with the stream of Alakananda river. But Shankar was firm in his resolve. He jumped in to that pond and in his very first attempt he was able to recover the stone idol of lord Vishnu. But a close examinations of the idol revealed it to be incomplete as its right portion was missing Shankar was convinced that the idol of Badrinavaryan (Lord Vishnu) could never have suffered mutilation and hence it might not be the genuine idol. With this thought in his mind he threw the idol again into the pond. Although he tried thrice each time he happened to recover that mutilated idol. While he has perplexed he seemed to hear a divine voice saying : "In this age Kaliyag this very image should be installed in the shrine." Following the divine instuructions Acharya Shankar (as he began to be called by this time) had that image installed in the temple with full Vedic rites. But he noticed that the Brahmins of that regions had virtually no knowledge of the Vedas and hence, he believed them to be incompetent to perform the worship of the idol with due rites. So he had this task assigned to Namboodaripad Brahmins (of his own gotra) from deep south and the arrangement still holds.

However, there is also section of scholars which claims that it was not due to any preference for him own gotra (clan) Brahman's that the Acharya assigned this task to Namboodaripad Brahmins but owing to his desire to augmenting the faith's solidarity in the whole country. If the brahmins from deep south were to be the priests of the temple situated almost at the northern border of our Aryavarta, certainly the whole country's cultural identity was to be fortified. We have already seen how Shankaracharya had revived the tradition of holding the Kumbh Melas with the same intention. In fact his idea was to not only redeem the Sanatan Dharma from the possible onslaughts from all directions but also make it self-sustaining and self-reviving by forming such in built devices in the faith itself. Appointing priests from far-off places and reviving the traditions of the Kumbh-like fair were his endeavours for keeping the faith dynamic and self rejuvenating.

Having finalised the arrangement of worship in the temple of lord Badrinarayan, he also established Jyotirmath (now known as Joshimath), putting it under the priestship of his disciple Totaka Charya.

It goes to the credit of Shankarachaya that wherever he went he created a semblance of order by arranging things in the proper way. Having made the region more conducive for his work he settled down to the main task for which he had come, viz. writing the commentary on the Brahma Sutras. He retired to a holy spot nearby where it was said that Sage Vyas had composed the Mahabharat. This ancient hermitage of Vedavyas is near Badrikashrama. Just below it is Keshava Prayaga where the river Alakananda meets the Keshavaganga. Here, there is a huge cave on the night side of which there is a temple of Saraswati, the goddess of tearing, and on the left, one of Lord Ganesha. For four solid years Shankarcharya lived in this cave alongwith his disciples, during which period he wrote his celebrated commentaries on the Brahma Sutra and Srimadbhagwat Gita. It was here that he wrote his interpretations of the Upanishads also.

It was here that yet another miracle had taken place. One day Sadanad had gone to the other bank of the river Alakananda for some work. Shankaracharya had no idea about his going on an errand. He happened to came on to this bank of Alakananda with his other disciple and unmindfully he yelled for Sadananda who heard him despite being the fast flowing river lying in between. Although there was a bridge on the river it was at some distance from the position Sadananda was at. So in the exuberance of his devotion to his guru he jumped into the river. As he placed his first step on to the water surface a lotus flower miraculously emerged there. As he proceeded further the lotus continued to appear just below his every step. And by the time he reached the other bank the river had a bridge of lotus flowers miraculously formed across it. He was so concerned for reporting to his master that he didn't see those flowers coming up. He immediately reached before the Master and asked him what was his command. The Master was so over joyed with Sadananda's overpowering devotion for him that he loudly praised his disciple's devotions before others. From that days Sadananda also came to be known as Padmapad-i.e having lotus flowers at his steps.

Having completed his major task of writing commentaries on the Brahma Sutra Shankaracharya visited the other centre of pilgrimage in the Himalayas. He first went to Kedarnath with his disciple. But the spot was much colder and more desolate than Badrinath. From there he went to Swargarohan mountain where the Pandavas had tarried before their going further up to the Swarga (heaven). Seeing the idyllic surroundings Shankaracharya decided to stay there for some days. But his disciples found the cold climes there to be unbearable. Through it made no difference to Shankar, his disciples were sorely troubled because of it. So in order to relieve them of their distress the Master, by his yogic power he happened to find a spot where a hot stream flowed. This hot water reservoir provided great relief to his disciples. Now Shankaracharya though called Master by his numerous disciples, was sixteen years of age. He also remembered that according to the prophesy made by the sage his term in the mortal world was fast drawing to a close. But as the Providence would have it, a strange event soon occurred which further enhanced his stay in the world.

One day at the day break when Shankar was enlightening his disciples with his commentary on the Brahma Sutra interpreted according to the principles of Monism or Advaitwad, there appeared an attracting Brahmin who asked the students as to what they were learning. They told him that they were learning what their guru had interpreted the Brahma Sutra from the point of view of Monism. The Brahmin said with a look of disbelief : "Who is there in this Kali Age who could fully grasp the mearing of the Brahma Sutra explained in the light of Advaitwad ? There are very terse Sutras composed by the sage Badarayan Vyas ? " Then the disciples of Shankar guided the Brahamin to their guru. On being intraduced, Shankaracharya said in all humility : "I heartily welcome anyone versed in the knowledge of Brahman Sutras. Although I don't profess mastery over the same yet I will try to answer you on the doubts you raise to the best of my ability." The Brahmin then posed some controversial points and Shankar put up the advait interpretation of the terse Sutras. The debate was quite animated and continued for seven weeks with out any decision. All the wise men that had assembled there were amazed at the depth of knowledge of both the persons on those Sutra. At last Shankar developed misgivings about that Brahmin's identity. Might not Badrayas Vyas be himself before him in disguise ? Then he requested the Brahaman to reveal his true identity. And to and behold, the great sage - Maharishi Vedavyas stood before him ! The sage asked Shankar to show him his commentary on the Sutras and having gone through he expressed his approval. Pleased with Shankar's work he blessed him, saying : "Now your life span will be doubled ? Now bring the Advaita Vedant to the knowledge of Kuamril Bhatt, the renowned pundit." Advising him to make Kumaril Bhatt accept his interpretations, the great sage departed.

Kumaril Bhatt was a famous sehokar, Shankaracharya had also heard about him from the pilgrims who also told him about Kumaril Bhatt's whereabouts. The scholar was living on the banks of sacred Triveni (Prayag) the holy spot at the confluence of the rivers Ganga and Jamuna. He immediately left with his deciple and going along the bank of Yamuna, he reached Prayag to meet Kumaril Bhatt.

Kumaril Bhatt had also become a legend in his life time. He was the great exponent of the orthodox system the 'purva-Mimamsa', the most celebrated Vedic school of those times. He was said to be an incarnation of Lord Subramanya, (Kartikeya, the younger son of

Lord Shiv). All this while he had been fighting single handedly to refute the Buddhist doctrine and re-establish the decaying Vedic faith. According to an unsubstantiated legend he had properly joined a Buddhist school in the garb of a Buddhist aspirant, in order to acquire better position to refute the Buddihst doctrines. It was a sort of sabotaging attempt. It is said that while he was thus getting familiar with the Buddhist philosophy in the 'Vihar', many of the monks would critise the Vedas in the course of their discussions which was too much for Kumaril and many a time he couldn't disguise his anger. The Buddhist grew suspicious with Kumaril's this behaviour. Knowing that he had obtained all knowledge of their religion for the sake of undermining it, they decided to kill him. Once they lured Kumaril into going atop the tallest building and pushed him down. Kumaril had realised their intention. As he fell down he kept on chanting a verse praying that if the Veda were true and eternal he should be saved. Although he didn't die, yet since he had doubted the truth of the Vedas, he was pierced by a stone, wounding his eye. Then he left the Bodh Vihar and went about propagating the Mimassa doctrine. No doubt the Mimasa doctrine also held the Vedas supreme but it went to the extent of asserting that there was no need of postulating a god, the Creator of the universe. This theory asserts that the Vedas are eternal and doesn't spring from a divine source. But the ritualist part is so much emphasised by the adherent of this theory that they even claim the futility of God and the deities who preside over the sacrifices. In there belief a deity is only an adjunt of the sacrifice. The merit of virtue accruing to one is only by the act and not due to the grace of the deities. It is the strict obveservance of the prescribed rituals that ensure merit to the person holding the sacrifice. The Minmansaks hold that even Moksha is attained only through the acts enjoined by the Vedas. But they also refute the Buddhist claims that Nirvana is the ultimate goal of any awakened soul. While Shankarcharya, in contrast to this belief, propounded the theory of Monism which claims that egoism is the greatest hindrance on the path of knowledge and hence emancipation. He maintained that, "abandon the notion of 'I in family clan, name, form and state of life." He is in agreement with the general Hindu concepts of Karma (works) rebirth and Moksha (liberation). But the point that he insists upon is that while good works are of assistance in securing favourable rebirth or a place in heaven true liberation can be only attained by knowledge of the Brahman. This knowledge is unattainable by the observance of rituals. He followed and advocated what is loosely called gyan marg i.e. the way of knowledge to realise god. More shall we be discussing about it ahead when we take up the theoretical part of Shankar's philosophy. This general discussion was necessitated by the intention of highlighting the difference between his concepts and that of Kumaril Bhatt.

As Shankarcharya reached Prayag he was told

that Kumarial Bhatt was about to immolate himself by entering a slow burning fire created by igniting paddy husk or 'Tushagni'. It was to expiate two major sins he believed he had committed Firstly, the deceit he had played on his Buddhist teachers and secondly his doubting the authenticity of the Vedas, for he had said : "if the Vedas were true"-when he was falling down. Shankar reached near Kumaril and tried his best to dissuade him from committing suicide by enlightening him about his Advait Vedant. Though he was attracted by Shankar's doctrine he was adamant that he must end his life since he had committed two acts of sacrilege. But before entering the Tushagnri he advised Shankar to go the Mahishmati Nagari[1] where the staunch Mimansaka, Mandan Misra lived and convince him about his doctrine of Monism. As Shankar bade him farewell Kumaril entered the paddy husk fire and ended his life.

Shankar left with his disciples for going to Mahismati nagar to win over Mandan Misra by his arguments rooted in Monism. it was this debate and eventually victory over Mandan Misra which finally established Shankarcharya as the leading scholar of his age.

1. Some accounts claim thaty the most famous debate between Shankarcharya and Mundan Misra had taken place in Kashi.

4. The Triumph of Advaitism

As Shankaracharya reached Mahishmati Nagari with his disciples he started enquiring about the staunch Mimansaka, Mandan Misra. One day when he was coming back after taking his bath in the river Narmada he enquired of the women returning with filled earthen pitchers as to where Mandan Misra lived. The women answered him in poetry. Beckoning toward a house nearly, they chanted a shloka which meant. "Where even the tame parrots prattles of philosophy; that is the house of Mandan Misra, the great sage."

Shankaracharya was greatly impressed by the hallowed nature of the place where even the birds would chant shlokas and even the common women would converse in poetry. He repaired straight to the sage's house. But it was closed from inside. It happened to be the Shraddh Day[1] of his departed father. Mandan Misra had shut the door of the house in order to be undisturbed during the ceremony. Vyasa and Jaimini were the two

---

1. The death day of the departed ancestor or the manes. On this day the dead are remerbered by offering food etc. to noble Brahmins.

Brahmins who had been nominated for the ceremony they were about to be feasted. But, notwithstanding the closed door, Shankar reached inside the house by his yogic power.

Now, Mandan Misra, a Karma-kandi (One who believed more in the rituals), had developed an anathema to the Sannyasi for whom he had unconcealed dislike. Seeing the young head-shaven ascetic standing before him especially when he was engaged in an important ceremony, he was enraged and asked disparagingly : "from where has emerged this Mundi (head shaven ascetic)?". In an attempt to put off Mandan Misra's anger, Shankaracharya replied in a humorous vein. "I am Mundi only from the head to neck." Though this answer made Mandan Misra all the more angry, Jaimini and Vyasa counselled patience and said that even the scripture advised feeding the homeless ascetics. Then Mandan Misra also invited Shanker to dine out of a leaf containing the consecrated food. Whereupon Shankar also told him the purpose of his arrival there. Mandan agreed, and after the 'Shraddha' ceremony the two great teachers-the Mimamsaka. Mandan and Advaitic Shankar-sat down for a religious disputation. By mutual agreement it was decided that Mandan's gifted wife-not less-learned-Sarasvani (also called Udayabharati) would act as the umpire. No doubt it was a delicate and quite embarrassing task for her, as one of the contestant's was her own husband. But wise as she was, she devised a method whereby she could not be accused of partiality. She declared that she would adorn each of the contestants with a garland, and that whose garland showed signs of fading at the end of the debate should be deemed to have been defeated.

Mandan Misra, confident of his victory looking at the adolescent Sannyasi also declared before the contest that should he be defeated he would gladly become of the follower of the victor and would do whatever the victor asked him to do. The news of the disputation, by that time had spread for and wide, drawing many pundits and scholars to hear the debate. This city of Mahishmati Nagari was a citadel of the learned scholars who thronged at the venue of the debate.

The debate, then, started with both sides putting question and counter questions with possible answers. However, it continued for many days. But at length, Mandan Misra began to lose his ground. The flowers in his garland showed district signs of witheredness.

At this juncture it is necessary to dilate a bit to explain the reason of a controversy said to have emerged at the stage. Many accounts aver that seeing her husband losing ground, the umpire, Saraswani, jumped into the fray on the plea that she had every night to defend her husband because she was his wife or Ardhangni (literally, holding half part of his husband). Although there was a murmur of protest since umpires are supposed to be impartial, yet Shankaracharya allowed her to intervene as if he was convinced of Saraswani's plea. As she took over from her husband her first question was on sex, the subject deemed to be very much part of Knowledge. Now Shankar was somewhat baffled as he had been celebate all this while and had no contact with any woman. Moreover, such contacts are totally taboo for the Sannyasis. But the question that Sarasvaṇi had asked could not be brushed aside because sex formed an imported branch of knowledge in India of that period, almost close to Vatsayan's time. This sage, Vatsayan's treatise on sex is still held to be a master-piece.

Then, Shankar was in a great fix. Either he would lose the battle or he must gain this kind of knowledge. But how a Sannyasi could have access to the sexual behaviour of human beings ? Thus thinking for a while he hit upon an idea. He asked for one month's time from Sarasvani, candidly explaining his predicament. "But what knowledge on sex would you gain in such a short time. Moreover you are a sannyasi ? How do you propose to do so ?"

"I won't spell out my modus operandi. But give me time and I would answer your question." Whereupon Saraswani allowed him to avail the desired time. Shankar promised to return in a month's time to her.

Here, it may be mentioned that those accounts that over Sarasvani coming for her husband's rescue also claim that this incident had taken place in Kashi and not in Mahishmati Nagari. So Shankaracharya repaired to the bank of the river Ganga to devise a method by which he could also he versed in sexology hut without breaking his vow of continence. While he was sitting on the famous Manikarnika Ghat of Kashi, even till now very much known for burning the dead almost non stop because it is generally held that cremation at this Ghat ensure the soul's entry into heaven. When Shankaracharya was sitting there brooding over his problem, he found a young prince's body being brought there followed by the royal attendants and a priest. Seeing that body Shankar thought of a trick to solve his problem. Before coming to Prayag he had also visited the Tantrik experts who happened to meet him on the way. While strongly dissuading them to stop human sacrifice he also learnt from them the art of reviving the dead. As he saw the young prince an idea occurred to him. He learnt from the royal attendants that their prince had died of snake bite. "Poor prince ! He got married only on the day before!" Shankar immediately decided to revive the prince's body by making his soul enter the body. Meanwhile he instructed his disciples to keep watch over his own life-less body till it got normally alive once again. As his soul entered the prince's body the latter woke up to life, to his relations great delight and wonder. Immediately they took the body back to the palace. It is said with the prince's wife's guidance who had unknowingly acted as a loyal wife, Shankaracharya sought the answer to the question Saraswani had asked. The moment he got the answer, his soul left that body and Shankar's body was revived to life with his soul's entering it again. The prince was again declared dead and duly cremated. But nobody from the palace could know as to why and how their prince was brought to life temporarily.

Getting the answer to the query related to sex, Shankar again reached near Sarasvani to resume the debate. Shanka's answer satisfied her and Shankar was declared the whiner. As was the condition put forth by none other but Mandan Misra himself he adopted Sannyas. He was initiated by Shankar who gave him a new name Sureshwaracharya and then Mandan Misra became a strong advocate of the Advaitic Vedanta. Sarasvani also followed her husband and joined Shankar's band of disciple. This victory symbolised a big triumph for Advait Vedant and established Shankar as an authority on philosophy all over the world.

While Shankar was still receiving the honours showered on him, his intuitive power told him that his mother's end was nigh. Since he had promised her mother to be near her at the time of her end, he left for Kaladi, his native place. Aryamba, his mother, was besides herself with joy seeing him so close to her. Shankar talked to her about Advaita in order to make her feel less sorry to quit this world. Soon her end came. Although those who take the vows of ascetism don't involve themselves in the mundane duties yet since Shankaracharya had made a vow that he would carry out his mother's funeral rites he decided to fulfil his promise against the simmering opposition in his native town. The local Brahmin were deadly against his doing its and hence they didn't cooperate with him. On the contrary, they displayed their unconcealed hostility. Left isolated and alone, Shankar is said to have caused fire to emerge from the right arm of his mother's dead body and this is how he is said to have performed the last rites of his mother.

But Shankar felt seething anger surging in his heart at his fellow Brahmins insensitivity. Instead of their appreciating the noble affection that Shankar had for his mother-like a worthy son ought to have-they were deriding him for having broken the vows of ascetism. Shankar grew furious at them and cursed them saying that thence their cremation ground would be their very homes. His curse had come true and some mysterious reason had made the Brahmin of Malabar cremate their dead in front of their dwelling places.

Shankar's this act, in fact, enshrined a lot of wisdom for the benefit of those dud scholars who refuse to see the spirit behind and ordained order by the scripture. Perhaps every faith in the world regards mother as equivalent to god. Didn't Rabindra Nath Tagore say. "since god couldn't be himself everywhere he created mother." Among all the worldly relations that between the child and the mother exceeds all mortal bandage. It is that relationship which is totally guileless and pure. Moreover, had Shankar not performed the last mites, wouldn't he have failed in his filial duties ? He showed that the Sannyasi is not a creature of stone and he has also a heart full of human kindness. Sannyas literally means even placement from every body, being the term created by joining (Sam + nyas) 'Sam', as we know, means even or uniform in Sanskrit and 'nyas' means placement. Hence the true definition of a Sannyasi is that he who is at uniform distance from everybody. A sannyasi should here his heart brimiming with love for everybody in direct contrast to a Grihastha (family man) whose source of affection are his chosen few relations. A sannyasi is one who lives ever in communion with eternity for he sees everything with the same view. Sannyasi doesn't mean an indifferent person passing through the world totally aloof from everybody. In fact the true sannyasi is a person having pious love for everyone.

By being so conscious of his insuppantable duty to his mother Shankar did what all sons worth their 'milk' should have done. He was also pioneer in showing his rare insight into the human relationship. There are thousands of saints renowned all over the world for their total detachment from murdane bonds but Shankaracharya's is the only example who having renounced the world for a divine cause yet didn't go indifferent or callous towards his worldly duties either.

Incidentally, Shankaracharya's this act reminds one of an episode related to Shiva ji's guru, Samarth Ramdas. It is said that long back, even before the advent of Shiva ji, in Maharashtra, the people had developed a false notion that devotion to god preceded over every mortal duty. They would not even care for their weeping infants at the time of a ritual worship. While in the evenings when the bells tolled loudly in the Aarti[1] of the chosen deities, the unattended infants cried at the top of their voices. An inherent belief behind this strange custom was also said to be this that in order to make the children emerge as brave persons, it was necessary to make them suffer the agony (mainly physical for children might not feel that poigrantly the mental agony !). No doubt it was some what inhuman to make the tender humanlings suffer so casually but this was what given much emphasis on during that period. In case the ladies found the men-folk's indifference towards children unbearable, a novel way of suppressing the children's cry was divised-the louder the children cried still louder the temple bells tolled.

But when Samarth Guru Ramdas saw this inhuman practice being perpetuated, he strongly objected to it. He is said to have impressed upon the misguided parents that a child symbolised the god to the closest perfection. "Why must you neglect the live god in preference over the dead image? While image is only a representation of the deity, a child in its guileless innocence is the deity him (or) her self," he is supposed to have argued. And then this strange custom was done away.

1. Holding a plate having lighted lamps and taking it round the idol while chanting mantras and songs.

This example was given to impress upon our reader that anything that is inhuman can't be good for divinity either. The rituals are mere appendages to manifest the spirit through action and not the spirit itself. This was the basic difference between the Mimansaka' approach and that of Shankaracharya.

Shankar's was one of those restless souls where no moment could be wasted in idle pursuit. Moreover, Shankar was wise enough to realise that he was surviving on borrowed time. While he had much less time at his disposal he had to accomplish a lot of important tasks. It was with this thought at the top of his mind that he kept on moving. He in his short age had gone round India thrice. Everywhere he went he preached the Advaita Doctrine which went much beyond the superficial ritualism and exposed the reality behind the phenomenal world. But his was not an iconoclastic endeavour. He never aimed at destroying any philosophical or religious systems. In fact his whole emphasis had ever been on solidifying them by winnowing chaff from the grains.

After the cremation of his mother he started his journey once again. This time he went to Maharashtra first and visited Shri Shaila or Shri Parvat. However this region had become a citadel of the Kapalik tantricks. Although these Tantriks were devotes of Lord Shiv they indulged in a peculiar and often macabre rites. Wearing garlands of human bones, frequenting cremation grounds and eating their food in human skulls were some of those rites. Wine and flesh formed their offering in worship. Human flesh was offered as oblation by them to the sacred fire, and they broke their fasts by drinking liquor from the hollow skulls of Brahmins. They believed that they acquired certain inpernatural powers by these gory practices. Shankaracharya lived with them for some time, trying to in inculcate in them the Advait faith. Although many of them were won over yet those who remained unaffected by Shankaracharya's lessons even conspired to kill him. Ugrabhairav was their leader who pretended to have been influenced by Shankar's discourses and became his disciple. One day he came to Shankar and said. "Master, a small obstacle has come in my way of acquiring mastery over an occult power. In order to cross this hurdle I have to offer the head of a king or some all-knowing Pundit. Who can be better suited Pundit than you yourself.1 So he pleased to offer your head for my mission."

Having guessed the man's vile intentions he said. "I never refuse come to my followers' help. You may come to me any day after your worship. But make sure that I am alone and also be careful about not letting my other disciples know about your sacrifice plan." Then I would gladly offer my head to you." Next day the kapalik came with a naked sword in his sand. But Shankar was lost in his samadhi. Meanwhile, Shankar's pet disciple, Padmapad, had seen all this through his yogic sight. Knowing what Ugrabhairav was about to do he chanted some especially charged incantations to propitiate Lord Narasimha. As the Kapalika raised his sword to severe Shankar's head, the deity in his ferocious half-man and half-lion form appeared and tore the Kapalika to pieces. Shankar was overjoyed at the vision of the Lord and composed Narasimha Strotra on the spot. The frightful deity's this act also discouraged other tantriks from continuing their gory practice and they readily accepted Shanka's doctrine of Advaitic Vedant. This event also made Shankar more popular and made his doctrine get wider publicity and acceptance.

Thereafter, Shankar continued his expedition all over the country, accompanied by his disciples. He went to Gokarna Kshetra (a holy spot near Goa) and then moving along he reached Harihar Kshetra. Although it was a predominantly Vaishnavite region, it was called Harihar which means of both : Lord Shiv and Lord Vishnu. Here yet another miraculous event took place which further strengthened Shankar's image as a divine person.

There was a small but famous temple which Shankar wanted to visit to pay his obeisance to the Lord. But seeing Shankar clad like a Shaiv Sannyasi-adorned with Vibhuti (Holy Ash) and garland of Rudraksha-the priest of the temple denied him entry since it was said to be a Vishnu temple. Then Shankar in his inimitable style explained to the temple authorities that whether one worshipped Lord Shiv or Lord Vishnu, He remained the same

Lord. After all the Lord didn't get changed with his devotees appearance. Eventually after lot of persuasion they opened the temple gate for Shankar. And lo and behold ! the idol appeared half of Lord Vishnu and half of Lord Shiv merging in one piece to justify the name of the region : Hari-Har (Vishnu-Shiv)

From Hari Har Kshetra Shankaracharya moved on to various other places. Accompanied by his disciples he happened to come to a place called Mukambi On the way he happened to show yet another miracle. It is said that he happened to come across a Brahmin couple bewailing over their only son's death. They had the dead body lying on their lap and they both were helplessly crying. Shankar was moved seeing their pathetic sight. He was so touched by their agony that invoking his yogic power he revived life in the dead boy. The couple was besides itself with joy and gratefully rushed to fall flat at Shankar's feel. The onlookers were amazed. Since Shankar never wanted his these powers to be publicised he rushed along, reaching Mukambi. The presiding goddess of the place Mukambika was believed to be very fierce. But he pacified the deity by establishing the Shree Chakra before her. Then moving along he reached Sribali which was the stronghold of only Agnihotri Brahmins. It was here he met one Prabhakar (already referred to) who had an imbecile, dumb son who was also of unsound mind. But when challenged by Shankar he began to speak like an erudite scholar, to the great amazement of the father, Prabhakar. Shankaryacharya made the boy his disciple. It was this boy who was to receive the title Hastamalaka (also referred to already and it means he has the whole world as clearly visible as a myrobalan fruit placed upon his palm).

Then Shankarcharya reached the spot he found to be divine during his last trip, where he sew a cobra sheltering the tiny frogs from scorching heat. This beautiful spot of Shringeri was on the bank of the famous river Tungabhadra, a tributary of the river Krishna. He found the place so charming that he had stayed at this place longest during his short span of life. He taught the Advaita Vedanta during this period particularly through his Bhashya or the commentaries. A large member of disciples gathered around him, among whom most noteworthy was Annandagiri. This disciple was not very bright being merely a boy having great devotion for his Master. But his other disciples ridiculed him for his slow-wit One day he had gone to wash his loin-cloth and so was late in attending his guru's discourse But the considerate Master waited for him even though his other disciples kept on saying that discourses had little meaning for Anandagiri as he didn't understand them at all. But as Anandagiri came, on being asked by his friends as to why he was late he started reciting his latest composition : 'Bhav Shankara Deshika Mey Sharanam' in the most different meter called 'Totaka'. This way Anandagiri not only proved his scholarship no less than other disciples of his master, but also pleased his Master as well. Delighted at his disciple's unexpected burst of poetic prowess, Shankar started calling him Totakacharya.

Having stayed at Shringeri for long, Shankaracharya again started his journey, this time to distant places, Prominent among them were Tirupathi, Chidambaram, Madhyarjuna, Rameshwaram, Tondi, Madurai, Anantashayana (the ancient name of Trivandrum), Nasik, Somnath, Dwarika, Ujjain, Mathura, and Kashmir

It was his trip to Kashmir that is of great significance. It is said that while staying with his disciples on the bank of river Ganga he heard about the hallowed Sharada peetha, a shrine in Kashmir. He came to know that the shrine was constructed in the form of a mandapa with four doorways and the gates which were supposed to open only when some extra ordinary scholar approached. Many learned men had tried to enter the shrine hut without success. When Shankar reached the southern doorway he encountered a member scholars who challenged him to a debate. Here Shankar demolished the arguments of the followers of other school of logic, like Nyaya, Vaisheshika, Sankhya and Poorva-Memansa and established his Advait Vedanta on a strong pedestal. Shankara demonstrated his wide knowledge and mastery of all these doctrine. The other scholars had to admit their defeat and the doors of the shrine automatically opened themselves. This way the fierce goddess also bestowed her favour on Shankar.

There are many traditional account about Shankar's stay in Kashmir. According to one when he came there a learned discussion with Abhinava Gupta-acharya on the topic of Shakti took place. Another tradition says that he lived near the present Shankaracharya temple and had a discussion on Shakti with a local priest in which he couldn't succeed to convince the other debater. After this he composed his famous : "Saundaryalahari". It is also said inspired by the knowledge displayed by a Brahmin girl, he composed his this poem.

Notwithstanding these varied accounts, what emerges from these is the glaring fact that Shankar's Kashmir visit was of great import and played a remarkable role in making the Advaitic Vedanta most popular and accepted school of metaphysics. His advent to Kashmir is commemorated by a impressive temple on thousand foot high hill, bearing his name till date[1].

From Kashmir, Shankaracharya visited Badrivana or Badnikashram where the episode relating to his digging out the idol of the temple of Badrinath had taken place.

A few miles south of Badrinath is the sacred spot

1. This hill, refrred to in Kalhan's classic 'Rajat tarangini' also, in near Srinagar. Allthough the Muslim call it 'Takht-i Sulaiman', the ancient temple on the hill, which survives to this day, dates from Shankar's visit and formed part of the original 'Jyestheshwar temple'.

Vishnuprayag. Shankar established a 'Math' here for the propagation of the Advait-teaching. His disciple-Annandagiri-also known as Totakacharya-was made incharge of that Math. It is situated now in Garhwal district and renowned as Jyotirmath or Joshimath. At Badrinath Shankar paid his homage to Govindacharya, his guru, and his guru's guru, Gaudacharyha who were both meditating in the Himalayas. After paying his tributes to them and receiving their blessing, Shankar decided to go to mount Kailash, the famous abode of Lord Shiv.

It is said that as he reached snow-clad Mount Kailash the Acharya had the vision of Lord Shiv. It is believed that the Lord had given him five crystal (sphatika) 'lingas' which were later consecrated by him at five holy places : the Moksha-Linga at the temple in Chidambaram, the Mukti-Linga at Kedarnath, the Vara-Linga at Nilakanth in Nepal, the Yoga-Linga at Kamkoti-Kanchi and the-Bhog-Linga at Shringeri. It is also claimed that Lord Shiv also advised him to spend his remaining days in preaching the Vedas and worshipping the Lingas thrice a day.

According to some accounts he also visited during the course of his expedition for establishing his doctrine Advaitism a number of holy spots as well. Included among them were Indraprastha, Ayodhya, Karnatak, Kam rupa (Assam), Kuru-kshetra, Gaya, Jagannathpuri, Nemisharnya (now called Nimisha in UP's Sitapur district), Prayag, Panchal Kshetra (central UP), Magadh, Rudra pur (UP), Venkata Chalanm (Bala ji) etc.

All these journeys-long, ardrous and performed in very difficult conditions-had started taking a heavy toll of his health. Although he was just beyond thirty he knew that his days were numbered. So he returned from the holy regions to the plains.

It won't be incorpruous to dilate at this stage on one's pre-knowledge about one's destiny. For a normal human being this is a hazard as it takes away the elemart of uncertainty and hence curiosity out of life. This makes life, to some extent, boring. May be, Shankaracharya had achieved so much during his short span of life that had he remained alive to complete normal human life span he would have felt bored !

Then Shankaracharya returned to the plains.

5. His Last Days

Returning from Kailash, Shankaracharya stayed for some time in Neelkantha Kshetra in Nepal (in modern times). While at Kailash he had known that the worship in the temple of Pasupathinath, was not being observed in an appropriate manner. Since Nepal had developed into a full fledged Buddhist centre by that time, people in general were becoming averse to traditional Hindu faith. Hence the worship in the five faced Pashupathinath Temple was suffering neglect. Shankaracharya went to Nepal with his disciples to revive people's faith in the traditional Hindu Dharma and enlighten them about his doctrine.

Nepal during that period was under the rule of the Hindu kings claiming their limage to Suryavansha (Solar Dynasty). It is said that the King Vrishdeva's son was baptised with the name Shankar to honour Acharya's visit to that mountainous state. During those times Nepal had its more stronger cultural ties with China than with India. Since China had the predominant influence of Buddhism, Nepal also had this effect. However, the Acharya's visit there had made a significant difference.

The Nepal King gave the Acharya a hearty welcome and showed him profound respect. The Acharya's forceful arguments won many people back to Hindu fold who were also drawn by Shankar's Advaitic Vedant. He also saw to it that proper arrangements were made for thc worship of Pashupathinath temple according to vedic rites. Since the learned Brahmins were not available there, he cnsured that his own castemen, the Namboodari Brahmins were appointed as the priest to conduct the worship the right way and this practice hold good to this date. Even now the priests of that famous temple are the Brahmins from far down south, from Kerala like they are in the temple of Badrinath. May be, some people smell parochialism in Shankaracharya's this act, since he ensured these lucrative ports for his own east Brahmins but they would he missing the basic point. Shankaracharya wanted learned and able person to conduct the worship of these hallowed temples. Since during that period the Vedic or Sanatan Dharma was declining in the face of the rampant Buddhism with the last recognised Hindu King-Harshvardhan- only about a century back showing his favour towards Buddhism, there were not many learned persons left in north who could perform worship as ordained by the ancient scriptures. Hence Acharya's bringing in experts from deep south. Moreover, it is not easy for a Keralita to agree to dwell hundreds of miles due north, in virtually alien surroundings for the cause of his faith. It goes to

Shankarcharya's credit that he managed to bring the Namboodari Brahmans so far north and they determinedly by continued the practice. Those who level this charge of parochialism on Shankar perhaps can't imagine what Shankar had achieved for the country's cultural and even political and religious ethos. If the Indian civilization has remained intact despite many onslaughts on it in the form of political, cultural and moral attacks it is because of such devoted sages like Shankaracharya. Now many Namboodari Brahmins have settled in Badrinath and Nepal to perform their traditional religious duties as initiated by this visionary sage. A 'Math' of Shankaracharya also exists now a little distance away from Pashupatinath Temple. The Acharya had also installed at Pashupathinath Temple one of the five crystal 'Lingas' which he had supposedly received from Lord Shiv Himself. The 'linga' installed here is called' 'Vara-Linga'. He also consecrated the idol of the goddess Mahatputri Sundari.

While staying in Nepal the Achrya also visited Kedarnath, where he installed the secured crystal-'Linga' called 'Mukti-Linga'. From Kedarnath he returned to Nepal and then went to the Gangetic valley, and coming on to the plains he reached Kashi via Amarda (Avadh). From Kashi he reached Onkar-ghat on the bank of Narmada river, and then to Puri (Jagannath) where he stayed for some time. Here he composed the famous 'Jagannath Ashtaka Strotra' and established the 'Purva

Amnayapeetha Math' (also called Govardhana Peetha) for spreading Advaitism. At this peetha he apponted his disciple Padmapad as the head priest.

From Puri he went to Shringeri, the place he seemed to have developed special liking for, and there he finally established 'Sharada Math', and installed yet another Linga under the name of Bhogachandra Maulishwar. The next place he visited was Chidambaram where he installed Moksha Linga in the famous shrine Natraj Temple. Here the local Brahmans, Dikshits, were entrusted with the worship of the holy linga.

Continuing his journey he reached Trichirapura to pay his homage at the shrine of Saugandhi-kuntalambika, situated on the Rock Temple. Here he had the text of the Saundaryalahiri engraved on the walls of the temple. From here Shankaracharya went to Shrirangam to pray Lord Ranganatha. It was at this place that he established the Janakarshana Yantra as he had established Dhanakarshan Yantra at Tirupathi. Thus continuing his unending travels, visiting on his way Rameshwaram, Tiruchandu and other places, the Acharya happened to reach the renowned sacred spot of south, Kanchi.

Here he stayed for some time. Kanchi has been a great centre of learning from the ancient times. Worshipping all the important temples of this region like. Sarvatirtha, VishnuKanchi, Hastagiri etc., he moved on after establishing Shankar Math which exists still there.

During his stay Shankara was able to persuade Rajasena, the King of Kanchi, to have the whole city redesigned in the form of Chakra. This was done and to this day it appears especially attractive. Worshipping the temple of the goddess Kamakshi, set in the middle, Shankar spent some time here. He also established yet another 'Peetha' : Kanchi Kamakoti and installed last of the remaining lingas he had received from Lord Shiv. The famous Sanskrit-poem 'Naishadhakavya' by Harsh refers about this crystal-linga in his description, saying that when crystal clear water was poured over the 'yoga-Linga', owing to the purity of the water and this object, linga, they appeared so intermingled in the view that the 'Linga' appeared to have been lost in that water.

Now Shankaracharya was about to complete his mortal age i.e. 32 years and his mission of establishing Advaitic Vendanta and reviving the Sanatan Dharma was almost complete. So it was time for him to depart. But there is no authentic record as to how his end came. While some say he abandoned his mortal frame at Kailash having accomplished his work and establishing the peetha at Shringiri, others say he quitted his mortal frame at Shringeri itself and yet another claims he did so at Kamakhi. Since there is so strong evidence in each assertion his place of death is not yet firmly established. But that is not important. What is of greater significance is what achieved during his short life span.

Person like Shankar come to the world very

rarely. For they are the messengers that come with a divine message. He is believe to be an incarnation of Lord Shiv who came with a specific mission. Whether he was a divine person or an ordinary mortal is not the point at issue. But what really makes him super human and god-like is the work accomplished by him in such a short span.

It is indeed difficult to imagine a person travelling so extensively about almost 1300 years back when the means of communication and transportation were hardly available. Only divine persons could to traverse the gigantic ice-cold mountains and the swollen rivers of the plains of Indian subcontinent, its difficult pathways and, at times, its almost inaccssible terraine, travelling mostly on foot. Imagine an adolescent travelling almost from the southern tip of the subcontinent and arranging for permanent and appropriate worship of the deities installed thousands of kms.away in the northern most rejoins of this huge tract called Aryavarta.

But his impact on the world can never wither away. His inspiring message is kept alive by the sacred fire which still burns in his 'Maths' and by the noble utterances contained in his ageless philosophy. His vision was universal and limitless which encompassed welfare of all animate and inanimate beings of this creation. His teachings can not have any end as they never had any beginning. It is a 'stream eterne' which runs on nourishing the awakened mind in every generation. For Shankar did not start anything new. In fact he only lifted the veil that was covering the gems of thought enshrined in the Upanishads. That Shankar was an avatar is vindicated by his achievements in such a short span of time. At an age when children play with toys he had not only understood the shallowness of the wordly existence but also renounced it. He is the rare example of one who remained a Sannyasi or a world-renouncing mendicant and yet discharged his worldly duties. And while doing all this he also enlightened people with his doctrine of Avaitism. Jugded by the concept and his interpretation he seems to beat even Kant, the famous philosopher of Europe, hollow. He established knowledge by thought and devotion by deeds. He was like that tiny smile that unites man with devotion with the brilliance of knowledge and man with dry knowledge with the flourish of deeply felt 'Rasa' of devotion. He had come in an age where mind and heart were compartmentalised into a sort of incompatible divisions, as the ace modern Hindi poet, Jai Shankar Prasad had described in his magnums opus 'Kamayani':

"Remote is knowledge and action different,
How can then heart's desire satisfied be,
Not they could meet, not could combine,
of life this is the great anamoly[1]."

[1] Translation by the author.

The Whole edifice of the Hindu thought was being dismantled by the incomplete comprehension; the rituals had no spirit and the spirit had no form. Then came this brilliant sage who united the two to make the whole thought again unassailable by vagaries of human understanding of the sacred text. In fact Shankaryacharya had not only revived the faith by his brilliant doctrine but had also revived the self-cleansing property of this ageless faith. Although much evidence is not available about Shankaracharya's reviving the Kumbha Fair tradition it appears very plausible that during his long travels he must have realised that the faith was getting polluted and stagnant because of lack of the agencies to purify it. It won't he incongruous to mention that these sort of big fairs are called 'Parva' in Sanskrit in which not only assembly at a holy 'tirtha' is mandatory alongwith taking bath in the holy streams, this was an occasion also to exchange views among the various high sages in order to amend the Dharma according to need of the time This torm 'Parva' appears to have been used allegorically. Like human body's nerve centres are called Parva which suggests as though these huge fair or congregation of the holy men signified the nerve centre of this civilisation. Revival of these Parvas accentuated the process self revival of the faith in the garb of these huge congregation at choosen places. Perhaps to this self-revival process initiated plausibly by Shankaracharya goes the credit of keeping this ancient civilisation still live and kicking. Otherwise there is no continent, subcontinent or large tracts of land in the rest of the world where a civilisation could keep its vigour and vitality almost ever vibrant.

It is in this light Shankaracharya emerges as a great reformer besides being an erudite scholar and able administrator. His achieve ment appears to get further magnified when one learns that all these feats he accomplished in only thirty two years. Covering the four corners of this Aryavarta with the four citadel of religious authority called the Peethas and interpreting the sacred text in a logical and laconic way he made sure that its mechanism for self-reguvenation remains intact and working. He is called the incarnation of Lord Shiv because the 'Shivrahasya' says "Shiv, the blue necked one, will out of his limitless grace incarnate himself many times to re-establish 'Dharma' and to help people."

6. Advaitic Vedanta : His interpretation

'Advait' is a technical term requiring etymological interpretations which the available space can't accommodate. Literally meaning 'non-dual' or 'indistinguishable', this terms has acquired a variety of meanings. Although the thought was existing earlier also it was powerfully brought into lime-light by Shankaracharya with his classic interpretation. Believed to be the apex of the ancient and modern India metaphysical logic, Advaitism or losely, monism stands on denial and not assertion. Hence it is obvious that the denied existence must be existing before the denial. In the ancient original thought there was no need to distinguish the two forms of god since he is basically one Later on, the need must have been felt of a symbol to guide the people owing to their growing strength which led to the entry of god with attributes. So we had two gods : one the original, basic and two, the one clad with shortcomings that came to be felt by the people in themselves from time to time. In fact the need of god exists to supplement the human limitation. No doubt this came to be the general belief- the god with form-of the people who had realised the capability of human existence Initially there was nothing but god. Hence whatever happened in that era happened exclusively by divine indication. Human effort was still not an element to be reckoned with. Then came the generation which had their palaces built by their foregathers and lots of riches to enjoy. So this era began to be effected by the worldly material wealth. But once you get the scale you will like to measure also. Hence the gradation in the worldly achievements and each class developing its individual likings. This was the era which felt the need of the 'divinity bursting forth' in a form which also led to the rise of the concept : god with form.

Having distinguished their separate entities the debate arose whether they contain the same element or not. Or that they contain two distinct elements each made with separate material. Whether the pot and the potter are made of different or same material ? So some believed in their duality some in their non duality and some in their interchangability in different forms. This reminds one the latest joke : First came the being with the head called the Moses who proclaimed that "follow the commandment received by me and all will be well with world." Next was the turn of holy Christ who declared : "follow my teachings and all will be well with the world." He was a man with heart who spoke of love. Then came Karl Marx who impressed upon the people that more important than head or heart was stomach. "So get your fill." The next one to appear was Singemund Freud who made everybody belive that that the source of all activation in a human body is something well below our stomachs. While conflicting influences were already working, there dawned on the horizon of human thought, Albert Einstein who confused every one thoroughly by mathematically declaring that everything is relative. So the civilisation is still confounded.

Shankaracharya it was who peached the doctrine of Advaitism to remove the confusion about 1300 years back. The Advaita Vedant of Shankar is probably one of the very few creeds which rests on no dogma. Unlike most other schools of Hinduism it believes uncompromisingly in a formless god which gives it at once an international status. Secondly, it makes pure knowledge its base. Thirdly, with its concept of 'Moksha' it provides a positive solution to the endless chains of births and deaths. Finally it tackles the problem of suffering in a novel and effective manner.

In fact Shankar's philosophy is not an intellectual gymnastics but goes to the core of life's ills. Why there is sorrow'?. He believes it is because of delusion which is twofold. Firstly in taking the real as unreal and deeming substance as the shwdow. Every day one sees people dying yet one never imagines that one will ever die. The Yaksha Prashna- that celebrated question that the Yaksha asked Yuddhishthar as mentioned in the Mahabbarat- still looms large before everybody. Why must all be so deluded as to believe that death would spare them ? Moreover, one knows that wealth brings more cares and anxieties than contentment yet one hankers after wealth. The force that makes us do all this is called Maya or Illusion It is a trap laid by god himself before his creations since Maya hides the truth or misrepresents it. The second reason for sorrow is attachment. We feel grieved when even our pet dog dies. We sadly grieve over when even an in animate thing like watch or ring is lost. It is chiefly because of attachment. Ironically, the thought that it is mine while initiating a process whose ultimate consummation is the development of the concept of 'Vasudhaiva Kutumbakam' also engenders the feeling of 'I-ness' which breeds sorrow. An English poem succinctly conveys this very thought when it says :

"When shall be I free ?
When shall my I cease to be "

Infact all these infatuations breed attachment which in turn breeds sorrow because whatever you get can also be lost. And even if that may not be lost you may be no more to posses it ! As mentained in Brihadaranyak Upanishad, once sage Yagyavalkya told his spiritually minded wife Maitreyi : "Verily, a husband is not dear that you may love the husband; but that you love the self, therefore your husband is dear to you, Your love for your husband is the consequence of your loving yourself. "Everything becomes dear to you because you hold yourself very dear to you." Yet another Upanishad claims : "Sarvam atmanah kamaya priya bhavati" or every one holds oneself very dear. It is your love for your own self that motivates you to perform any action. Suppose you love your son. Then whatever you do for him is verily your doing to satisfy your own self. That son is the beneficiary not because of your love to him but because of your love to self. Crudely proclaimed, a western thinker opined the same thought when he said : "love for progeny is the natural consequence of the certitude of death. Had man been immortal he wouldn't have loved his son or other issues." It is because he wants the traces of his identity to remain even after his death that he loves his descendants.

As is natural this feeling of I-ness breeds egoism. Shankar considered egoism to be the greatest hindrance on the path of knowledge and emancipation. In his 'Vivekachudamani' he proclaims " abandon the notion of "I" in family clan, name, form and state of life". In the same book he says " " The great 'Ahankar' even though apparently cut down to its roots, will, if excited only for a moment by the mind, come to life again and cause a hundred distractions, just as during the rain, clouds are scattered about the storm."

It is this I-ness or ego sense that creates a lot of fetters around one self. In a She'r a modern Urdu poet : Shahid Holipuravi, claims :

"Naam hai kaum hai valdeeyat hai
Dost Abbaab hain shaksheeyat hai
Kaise kaha doon ki azaad hoon main
Kya ye bande silasil naheen hain ?"

Meaning that I have a name, a nationality, the parentage; friends, relation and a distinct personality. How can I say that I am free. Don't these constitute the links of the chain that fetters me ?"

Shankar claims that the other factor that hampers one's progress to wards knowledge is 'Avidya' or ignorance. Avidya literally means that agency or impression which manifests the world appearance. What even one seen around him, whatever one feels or imagines, in fact everything except Brahman or the Absolute-the entire world of thought, creatures and objects-is due to this avidya. Of course if takes a lot of pains to realise that whatever you know or realise is false ? In his famous creation 'Aparokshanubhooti' (i.e. indirect or deductive realisation) Shankar says : "The universe though it be a subject of daily experience and the object of our constant intercourse, is unreal like a dream, in as much as its existence even in the moments following its birth is not provable." This is the same Kantian principle about the notion of the things. A brick may appear like a brick because we know that any object with this shape or look is a brick. This is our notion. But while Kant claims the fallacy in the notion can't be rectified, Shankar believed it could.

In fact the concept " Brahman satyam jagat mithya " is, to a great extent, is a universal concept. While Shakespeare says. " We are such stuff/ As dreams are made on , and our little life is rounded with a sleep."

(the 'Tempest') Shelley in his celebrated 'Prometheus Unbound ' says " Death is the veil which those who call life : they sleep and it is lifted ."

In fact what is real and what is unreal very much depends on individual experience. Knowing that dreams are unreal , at times we get up in the middle of a night with a heart pounding and sweating profusely seeing a night mare . This is so when we are fully conscious of the fact before dreaming and after dreaming that dreams are unreal and false. Even this consciousness at times remains that whatever we are seeing is a dream is an impossible event like one's seeing in dream one's talking to his father who died ten year ago. Or, seeing one's son talking to one's father when even in the dream one realises that both have not existed in this mortal world simultaneously. But despite this consciousness we get affected by the dream. And it may is happen that we may see an event occurring before one's eyes in this conscious world may it but not be real. Like a play getting enacted before you and you may cry seeing in the Ram Lila at Ram's wailing over Lakshman's unconscious body, although all the viewers of the play are sure that Lakshman will not die. In this context there is a subtle difference between the two stages. One's dreaming and one's watching a play. While watching the play one's conscious brain is fully alert and though one might cry over Ram's wailing over Lakshman's unconscious body, the sentiment of empathy which wells tears in one's eyes may be a fleeting one. This is no lasting agony in such viewing. But in the dream the agony is of lasting impact. Here the pain is real following seeing a heart rending scene-like death of one's near and dear one. So when the Supreme Being incarnates Himself He doesn't feel pain or is affected by the mortal grief. Only because He is conscious. But man feels the pain because he is not conscious that this world is also-as Shakespeare observes : "a walking shadow, a poor player that struts and frets his hour upon the stage. And then he is heard no more : (for life) is a tale told by an idiot, full of sound and fury signifying nothing"

But like other saints Shankar did not deny the world's existence. He only said that it was not real in the sense that we are helpless spectator in all that happens in it just as the dreamer haplessly dreams his dreams. The kind of things he considered to be really false were those which have no existence altogether, as for example ,'a barren woman's son. It is obvious that a barren woman in can conceive a son only her dream or in the realm of imagination" This point is frequently explained in the Upanishads by giving the example of a man mistaking a rope for a snake. Here too, going by Kant's reasoning the snake has some basis because its idea exists till the error is not cleared in the beholder's mind. Till then the snake has an existence in the sense that it creates the impression of a real snake.

But Shanker denies that the world is wholly illusory. In one of his Brahma-Sutra Bhashyas, the learned sage claims that the world is 'na swapnavat' (not of the nature of the dreams). The world of name and form is unreal only in the sense that it affects different minds differently. As the famous urdu poet Jigar Muradabadi says :

Use saiyyad ne kuchh, gul ne kuchh bulbul ne kuchh samajha

Chaman men kitni maaneekhez thee ek khamoshi meri,"

[How meaningful was my silence in the garden with the gardener, flowers and birds deriving their own meaning out of it]

Hence reality as observed by the senses or through them perceived by the conscious mind is illusory. Shankar believes that as far as absolute truth is concerned it is only the Absolute. And the knowledge that Atman (soul) can't be different form Parmatama (God) is what the real gyan or knowledge is . For Shankar knowledge of Brahma is the real gyan, and not the scholarly knowledge.

The Vedanta considers Brahman and Atman to be of the same nature, and so we find the terms interchangeable. The Absolute is beyond definition. Hence the vedas proclaim : Neti..... Neti..... (not this ....not this) for it is much more than what comprehended. It is Sat-Chita -Anand (Truly Conscious Bliss). However Shankar's concept of Brahman was greeted with initial opposition. The argument was that if it was beginningless and without attributes how could it be the cause of the world ? Therefore he conceived of Brahman as both attributeless (Nirguna) as well as with attributes (Sagun).

These, however, are only two aspects of Brahman and it doesn't mean that there are two Brahmans. The need for having the two aspects of Brahman, was very succinctly put by Ghalib, the Urdu poet par excellence.

Jab ki tujh bin nahin kai maujood
Phir ye hangama Ei Khuda kya hai ?

[When no one exists but, you, O god, how come this creation survives?] In this light Shankar's doctrine can be summarised as : The Absolute or Brahma is the sole entity and every thing else is false and unreal including the world and secondly the soul in also no different form the Absolute.

But that Atman is indistinguishable from Paramatman or both have the identical element of consciousness is not everybody's cup of tea. For that the Atman must rid itself of those infatuations or pollutions that defile its vision . This realisation can come only is a flash when one's soul is free from egoism, arrogance , sense desires. greed, attachment, avarice, cruelty, falsehood and a host of similar other vices. Although Shankar is in agreement with the general Hindu concept of 'Karma' (action), rebirth and Moksha, he goes ahead to claim that while good works are of assistance in securing a favourable rebirth or place is heaven, true liberation can only be attained by the pure knowledge i.e. realisation of Brahman In his celebrated 'Viveka Chudamani' he claims categorically that one may study the neriptures propitiate gods by sacrifices, perform all ordained religious ceremonies yet he can't attain salvation no matter he gets a hundred life. It is because if the Atman's vision is clouded by various vices how can it see the truth ? In order to get a clear view of yourself not only your mirror should be unsullied your face and your eyes should also be with out any blemish. Hence it is obvious that the Atman will have to do great efforts to clear all these sloughs of unreality before getting the true vision. This certainly can't be achieved in one life time or even in many life times. The Bhagwat Gita warns : " hardly anyone perceives the Atman (soul) as marvelling, scarce another speaks of it as such while there are some who know it not even on hearing of it[1]" Moving about the rest and observing a ritnal without realising the purpose behind it is like chanting the name liue a parrot : This realisation comes after many similer' efforts performed by the awakened person and when it dawns you realise that knowing the truth you have said it, knowing the beauty you have served it and knowing the good you have done it.

But Shankarecharya was not against devotion although he favoured enlightened devotion like an Urdu couplet's line says :

Saqi sharab dey mujhe
kah kar sharab hai

[O my beloved wine server! Give me the wine by telling it that it is wine]

1. 'Srimad bhagwat Gita', chapter ii, verse 29

When the Urdu poet who wrote this line was asked as to where was the sense in this line? 'give me the wine by telling it that it is wine.' Isn't it obvious ? After all when you give it and I see it, where is the sense in your telling it also. The poet replied that he said it because he wanted satiation of his all sensual perception : that it is wine is what one can see ; that it would be also tasted by one and hence the skin or touch sense would also be satiated. This way while all senses receive their satiation by the cup of the wine it is only the audio sense that is deprived of its pleasure. " Hence the request to give it after telling what is it."
In other words, Shankeracharay wanted devotees to be enlightened enough to know the entity they worship. Crudely speaking, you night be barking up the wrong tree! So he wasn't an atheist or against theism. The formless God assumes form as Ishwar for his devotees . Like Goswami Tulsidas has claimed in his celebrated magnum opus," Sriramacharitamanas':

"Jaki rahee bhavana jaisee !
Prabbu murat dekhi tin taisee"

[One worships one's god in accordance with one's perception]

The two 'kinds' of God are as identical as water or snow or ice. Both are made of two molecules of hydrogen and one molecules of oxygen. The difference in their appearance results out of the influence of the external conditions. One cannot see electricity but we know its presence when it lights a bulb or runs a fan. In its external manifestations or internal presence it is the same entity.

Going by the same argument it is also obvious that there is no gradation in these two kinds of the Supreme Entity. That snow is higher or water is lower might be a geographical fact hut not a qualitative difference. Water is water and snow or ice is also water. May be in hot climes ice might fetch better value but it is due to the external conditions. Internally there is no elemental or basic difference. A bulb lighting the chapel hall cannot claim superiority over the bulb lighting the bath room. It is the external requirements that change its appearance to suit their purpose. So, too, it is with the formless Brahman and Brahman with form. Shankaracharya didn't belittle faith and devotion of the sincere kind. His whole life makes it self-evident. But he had no patience with the ignorant worshippers. He might forgive the innocent and would like to enlighten that person For that follow has not yet developed discernment . But those with discernment tend to be ignorant out of their desire to show their devotion more flamboyantly had no pardon from Shankar. Guru Nanak also expressed the same thought when he said that mere outer garment cannot please Him . And those who tend to cheat Him languish in this mundane. ocean by repeatedly coming back to it.

Unlike the earlier tradition Shankar never cared to limit this knowledge of the Ultimate to any particular caste or community . He only said that they who possess discernment between the eternal and the transistory , renunciation and indulgence and have longing for liberation are entitled to aspire to receive it. He insisted that this discernment can be cultivated by getting tranquility of the mind , restraint for sensual attraction , resignation to the divine will, capacity to meditate and capability of having an unwaivering faith.

Hence Shankar's doctrine is also beyond any man made limitation and truly a catholic concept in the widest meaning possible. There is no dogma for dogma in his doctrine.

Shankar believed that Brahman and liberation are identical terms : "Brahman eva hi muktiavastha" That liberation is realisation of Brahman has been a central thought of the entire Hindu thought. Goswami tulsidas says :

Tehi janahu jehi deu janaayee |
Jaanat tumahi tumahi hoi jaayee. ||

[He knows you whom you wish to be enlightened about yourself. But the moment he knows you becomes you yourself]

And this liberation is not possible merely by action although religious practises, being an auxiliary means of acquiring knowledge, destroy the obstacles in the way- the greatest of which are arrogance, egoism and the lure of senses - and hence it be necessary initially to discipline your mind. It is said that Valmiki became such a great devotee of Ram by chanting the name in the reverse way (Mara)[1] . In his case initiation was essential even though with a wrong pronunciation in order to make him associatied with Ram. In fact you get devoted to a form easily because there is something before you to concentrate on. But all actions related to even devotion are binding because they must bear fruit in the shape of enjoyment or suffering. However, for the man who has attained knowledge there is no longer prescribed action. Kabeer , the ace Medieval poet says:

" Man mast hua tal kya bole
Hansa paayo mansarovar
Taal - talaiyya kya dole?"

[When the mind attained bliss what should it say? When a swans gets to Mansarovar way should it hanker after small ponds and tarns ?] It is all the same when such liberated person works or not . If he does the action will not cling to him. Imfact a action has two variety . One is the 'Prarabdha Action ' which may be likened to an arrow which has already been shot from the bow and it must find its target. The other kind is 'Sanchita karmas' They are in store but have not yet begun to bear fruit. The 'Brahma Sutra' claims that - since the attainment of Brahman destroys only the Sanchita Karmas - of the knower of Brahman only those of the former actions that have yet to begin bearing fruits (anaarabdha). That is why body of such a person continues to exist for a while out of sheer inertia just as a potter's wheel goes on re-

1. In devanagari script

volving even when the vessel it supported is complete . Such a knower of Brahman is not deceived by Maya for he sees through this illusion the ultimate reality. A person attains complete liberation when the Sanchita Karmas have been destroyed by knowledge of Brahman and the Prarabddha ones have borne fruit. Then the person is like the river that has reached the ocean, dissolved its existence and become the ocean itself. A Ghalib says in his famous couplet :

"Asle shubood-e-shahid-e- mashhood ek hai

Hairan hoon phir mushahida hai kis hisab men ?"

Meaning, when the view, the viewed and the observation itself are identical who is watching whom ?

There is no doubt that Shankar's exposition of the Advaitic Vedanta is monumental. The term Vedant originally meant to be the conclusion of the Vedas as far as the metaphysical 'Vision' is concerned. These teachings were recaptitulated in the 'Brahma Sutras' on which Shankar's ommentary is peerless. To establish this theory of Advaitic Vedant which may be loosely rendered as that Vedic conclusion that He is not dual, he wrote many looks which have been briefly mentioned in the coming chapter.

7. Famous works of Shankaracharya

Antiquity and wide range of erudition are the two most stumbling blocks when one attempts to select the works written by Shankaracharya. He was a sort of pioneer in this field. He not only administered different Peethas he had established but also wrote commentaries, hymns, shlokas on a variety of subjects. To confound the matters still more the other chief priests of the religious seats also added their creation to his works, allegedly writing with the same name. Hence it is very difficult to pin-point the works truly created by him Infact there are more than two hundred works which bear the name of Shankaracharya. Also there have been a number of Acharyas of this name who have headed the various 'Maths' which went on multiplying all these years since the advent of the original Shankaracharya. What adds to the confusion is the fact that nearly all of these head-priest of the Math claimed their guru to be Govindapad.

Moreover, it was a common practice with the ancient Hindu authors to create their works namelesly.

The authors were not supposed to write or append their names with their creations. It was only from about 1000 AD that the created works began to bear the author's name. Hence going by the available practice Shankar never mentioned his name any where. In fact the only means available to select his works with any degree of authenticity is by studying the contents and analysing the personal stamp in the diction and style. A classic example is the famous creation :"Devyapar-adhakshmapan strotra", believed generally and widely to be written by Shankaracharya. Going even by the style, diction and contents it appears very much a poem by him. But its fifth shloka has a line :

"Parytyktā devā vividhavidhisewā kulatayā

Mayapanchāsheete radhikamapaneete to vayasi"

Now concentrate on 'Mayapanchasheete...' which literally means that "I have completed more than eighty five years...!" How can this be ever written by Shankaracharya who lived not beyond thirty two by any account ? Although the contents indicate it to be his creation since his emotional attachment to his mother is well known and the burden of this poem asserts that a son could be unworthy but never a mother, yet owing to that time referred to above it cannot be attributed to him. There are many such examples wherein either the contents of the creation appear to be his but not the style and diction or vice-versa.

However, generally adopted method of ascertaining whether a creation is genuinely his or not is his typical style. His language combines lucidity with directness. It is generally simple unconvoluted and direct. Applying these standards mutatis mutandis the scholars have selected the following works as to be has genuine creations.

(i) Commentaries : His commentaries on the 'Brahma Sutra' and 'Bhagwad Gita' head this list which are considered to be the most powerful exposition of these source books. In fact these became so renowned that the very term 'Vedanta' came to be known as Vedanta of Shankaracharya. As has been explained before Brahma Sutra are the metaphysical essence of the Vedic teaching which has also been expounded by the Upanishads. 'Sutra's' literally mean the threads or strings. Thus aphorisms are short pithy sayings which thread together various ideas. It is believed that Badarayan Vyas was the first to compile and explain the Brahma Sutra.

The second book on which Shankar's commentary is reckoned to be outstanding is the celebrated 'Srimadbhagwatgita'. His commentary starts with the eleventh verse of the second Chapter in which he emphasises the role of knowledge in bringing liberation. Comparing the various views of the other commentators he gives clear exposition of his own views. As has been his considered opinion Shankar's stress is on knowledge of Brahman. He disagreed with those who justified animal sacrifice on the plea that Lord Krishna had exhorted Arjuna to kill his enemies. His argument was that the Lord never sanctified killing but only said that while doing one's duty one should not flinch killing his near and dear ones if they presented themselves as the obstacles.

His commentaries on Upanishads are also famous. He interpreted the meaning of twelve Upanishads which include Kena, Isha, Katha, Mundaka, Mandukya, Tattariya, Aitreya, Chhandogya to name a few important ones. As is obvious he interpreted them in accordance with his own doctrine establishing the supremacy of knowledge.

Apart from these he had also written commentaries on Vishnusahastranam, Sanatsujatiya and the like.

2. The Hymns : Besides being a brilliant scholar Shankaracharya was also a class poet. His hymns to the various gods and goddess reveal the devotional side of his nature. Famous in this category are 'Ananda Lahiri' 'Govindashtaka', 'Dakshinamurti-Strota', 'Manasollas', 'Dasha-sloki', 'Dwadash-panjerika', 'Shat padi', 'Charpart-panjarika', 'Manisha panchaka', 'Shivabhuganga-Prayata'. Some of these have been translated in English and Hindi in prose which are included in our translation section.

3. Advaitic works : Shankar had written them to establish his doctrine. Popular among these are :

'Aparopshanubhuti' (Self-Realisation) 'Atma-bodha' (Self-knowledge), 'Upadeshashastri', 'Panchikaranam', 'Prabodha Sudhakar', Vakya-Vritti', 'Vivekachudamani' Some of these have already been refered to in the preceding pages. In fact there are scores of other such creation whose anthorship is attributed to Shankar but on close examination they were not found authentic as there are as many interpolation as to confuse the basic thought. May be they are his disciples' creations.

4. His creation on Tantra Shashtra : Notwithstanding his deprecating the debased form of Tantrik observance consisting of human sacrifices he was not averse to the basic thought behind this kind of worship. He had himself said that the worship of Shakti is the same as Advaitic realisation. He differed with the form but not with the spirit behind Tantra philosophy.

Most popular in this category is his oft quated 'Saundaryalahari' which as the legend goes, was handed over to him by no one else but Lord Shankar at Kailash Mount. It contains 100 verses, the first 41 of which deal with the practice of Tantra while the remaining ones describe the grace and divine charm of the goddess Bhagwati who is believed to reside with in 'six chakras[1]'. No matter what the legend is, the clarity and felicity of

[1] The Tantra school of worship believes them to be existing in the hollow of the body's spinal column They are mulādhārā (earth) swadisthāna (water), manipurā (fire), anāhata (air), vishuddhā (ether) and ajnā (psychic) which open when the aspirant attains Siddhi.

language with which serene ideas are expressed leave no doubt about Shankaracharya's authorship. 'Prapanchasara' is also believed to be his Tantrik creation although it is subject to controversy about Shankar being its author.

The above mentioned brief reference about his major works is by no means comprehensive but our idea is to give the readers a general idea about Shankar's creative ability. One gets baffled at his such a wide range of knowledge and his erudition to succinctly put that knowledge in verse despite his being so mobile during his short sojourn on the earth. Imagine his achieving all these feats in such a short span of life. And he achieved all this when one had to write only in long hand on scrolls which had been a very cumber-some process. Even though only half of the works ascribed to him may have authentically issued from his pen there is no denying the fact that they contain such gems as might pale the most brilliant philosophical works into insignificance.

8. The holy Spots and Places Associated with Shankaracharya's Name

Although briefly all these places have been mentioned in the chapters before, the details are now being given to make the reader know their modern location as also to judge how far and frequent were this extra ordinary sage's visits in that ancient time.

(i) Badrinath : On the confluence of Rishiganga and Alakananda rivers lies Badrinath, one of the four Dhams (centres) founded by Adi Shankaracharya. It is 296 km. from Rishikesh. (U.P.), a modern town now. It is believed that the idol of Badrinath was installed in the present 15 metres high imposing temple by Adi Shankaracharya. Badrinath takes its name after "badri"-the wild berries-which once grew here in plenty.

This great shrine of Badrinath, amidst snows and solitude, is connected from Rishikesh from where regular bus service and taxis are available. For stay at Badridham and other sacred places in the region, there are now many Dharmashalas, Tourist Bungalows, PWD inspection Houses, Hotels and Rest Houses.

(ii) Joshimath : Situated at 1874 metres height from the sea-level, it is a very important town in terms of trade and religion. It is here that Adi Shankaracharya attained enlightenment and established one of the four Peetha (a kind of monastery) Narsingh temple and Navdurga temple are other famous shrines. Badrinarain, the deity, is worshipped at Narasimha Temple during winters when Badrinath Temple remains closed (between Nov. and April) At Joshimath one of the four present Shankaracharyas still reside to regulate Vedic Dharma. It is connected by bus routes from Rishikesh.

(iii) Shankaracharya Hill at Srinagar (Kashmir) : South of the Dal Lake, behind the Boulevard, rich in legend and lore is this famous Hill which has a temple atop it. The present shrine is of later origin. About a millennium and a half back Adi Shankaracharya had visited this spot. Then Abhinavgupta was the Acharya of an educational institution. It was here that he met Shankaracharya and held a long philosophical and religious dialogue. Since the visit of Shankaracharya this hill came to be associated with his name. Those who are willing to visit this sacred place should make Srinagar their base which is well connected by air and land route with the rest of the country.

(iv) Sharadamath At Dwarikapuri In Kathiawad (Gujrat) : Dwarikapuri, a famous pilgrims centre for the Hindus where Adi Shankaracharya had established one of the Peethas in 8th Century A Shankaryacharya still reigns here. These are regular state bus scrvices to Dwarika from various major towns in the region.

(v) Sringeri (Shringeri) : East of Udipi in Karnatak lies this holy Math. Adi Shankaracharya's this favourite spot had a Peetha where a Shankaracharya still reigns. Situated on the bank of the river Tungabhadra it is still an important citadel of the Advait philosophy, the doctrine of Shankaracharya. This place is well connected with the state's capital, Bangalore, by rail and road routes.

(vi) Govardhan Math at Jagannatha Puri (Orissa) : This is the fourth cardinal point which has a Math established by Shankaracharya and still a Shankaracharya reigns here. Puri is otherwise a very famous religious centre for the devotes of the Krishna cult. Puri is just 65kms. from the state capital and well connected by a verity of means of transport.

(vii) Tirupati : This famous religious centre in Andhra pradesh is also associated with Shankaracharya's name. According to tradition he sang Lord Tirupati's praises in the famous verses known as the 'Vishnupadadi Strotam". He also consecrated and installed there the Dhanakarshan Yantra.

(viii) Chidambaram : Sixty eight Kms. further south of Pondicherry towards Tanjore is a magnificent complex of temples at Chidambaram. Shankara visited this place to pay his respect to Lord Chidambaram and had consecrated the Panchakshara Yantra or the Yantra with five sacred letters. According to tradition, he visited the place in the temple where his guru's guru, namely Gaudapada learnt the Mahabhashya from Patanjali.

(ix) Madhyarjuna : This sacred place situated on the southern bank of the Kaveri river, is, in modern times known as Tiruvidaimarudur. It is in the middle of Tanjur district of Tamilnadu. Shankar is said to have visited this place on his way to Rameshwaram where a miracle had happened. When Shankar entered the temple it was his wish that the great Linga in it should of itself declare the truth of Advaita and as he prayed the god himself appeared from the Linga and proclaimed that Advaita alone is truth.

(x) Rameshwarm : This famous sacred spot on the southern most tip of India was visited by Shankaracharya where he worshipped the sacred image of Ramanatha with holy Ganga water.

(xi) Tondi (or Tondipuri) : From Rameshwara Shankar visited this nearby spot where he paid his homage to Ganesh and sang his praises in the Ganesh Pancharatanamala.

(xii) Madurai : It was in the renowned shrine of

this religious town, Meenakshi Temple that Shankaracharya composed his famous poem 'Meenakshi Pancharatrna Strotram' to express his feeling for this much revered goddess.

(xiii) Anantashayanam : This is the ancient name of the famous city Trivandrum. Shankaracharya had visited this famous citadel of Vaishanavite worshippers. Having stayed there for about a fortnight he managed to make many Vaishnavite the follower of his Advaita doctrine.

(xiv) Nasik : This place, hallowed in the Rama lore where the demoness Shurpanakha's nose was cut by Ram's younger brother Lakshman, was also visited by Shankaracharya on his way to Kailash Mount. Here he worshipped Lord Triambakeshwar. This visit is alluded to in the well known 'Dwadashlinga Strotram'

(xv) Somnath : A renowned centre of the Shaivites this was already a famous centre of pilgrimage when Shankar visited it It was from here that he visited Dwarka and established his Math, making his disciple Hastamalaka the first Acharya.

(xvi) Ujjain : Held to be one of the great Shaivite places of pilgrimage from a hoary past and having one of the twelve sacred Lingas, Shankar had stayed here for some time, worshipping in Mahakaleshwara and Maha Chandi temples. Here he also held a debate with one of the most powerful Tantrik, Bhairava and defeated him. A number of Jains, Buddiests and the followers of the Chārvāk school (hedonists) were also overwhelmed by Shankar's doctrine of Advaitism.

(xvii) Mathura : Since Shankar's family deity was Lord Krishna, he had especial charm for this place. While he was here he also visited Gokul and Vrindavan. From here Shankar had gone to Mayapuri, a place near modern Haradwar.

(xviii) Kailash : It was here that Shankar is believed to have received the Sphatik Linga's from Lord Shiv. This most hallowed abode of Lord Shiv is still not easily accesible being part of the territory controlled by China.

These were the places mentioned mostly in Shankar's works, although he might have visited many more. Travelling all through almost on foot, it is amazing that he had covered these far off places in his very short span of life. The Achrya had also visited Holy Temple of Pasupatinath in Kathmandu Nepal whose details have been given in the earlier chapters. Included in this Nepal itinerary was also his visit to Kedarnath.

It appears he was working with great dedication. Visiting all these places he almost culturally united the whole of Aryavarta. The four Peethas established by him are like four strong citadels of a unique cultural and religious faith. India owes a lot to such peripatetic saints who saw to it that this tract of land remained united by some sort of common link.

9. A Visionary Saint Beyond Compare

Shankaracharya was not only a pioneer among the saints of comparatively modern age, but also the best specimen of that order. Earlier saints or the Rishis or Munis (sages) as they were called, moved in a different realm clouded by a mythological sheen. There were Narad, Vyas, Angira and scores of the divine persons who moved freely at will and for whom no place was inaccessible. But in Shankaracharya we have a saint whose accomplishments even though judged by the mundane measures place him at a divine pedestal. Owing to being of a comparatively recent origin not much of the divinity cover could be placed over him. That he came to be reckoned as an incarnation of Lord Shiv is not corroborated by any solid evidence barring apocryphal legends but when we compare his achievements in such a short span by even modern standards we can't keep ourselves from searching a divine spark in him, for humanly all this was not achievable by anyone living for only 32 years.

Moreover, he had a vision in his mind. He wanted to establish Sannyasi's reputation at par with the old sages who ever thought of society's welfare even while living away from it; who saw to it that moral values didn't fall and if they did it was they who summoned the divine incarnations to set right the global order. Interestingly, it is claimed by our scriptures that while the sages or seers could suffer the agony with the distressed they were not competent to remove the cause of the agony. The brightest example to vindicate the truth is mentioned in the period offered by the time just before Lord Ram's incarnation. The demons had become so strong that coming from their citadel in deep south-Lanka, they could penetrate the northern hold of civilised human kings as deep as upto the passage between Ayodhya and north Bihar for, it was the place sage Vishwamitra was performing his yagyas (sacrifices) which were being disturbed by the demons. It was to get relief from this demoniac-disturbance that Vishwanita had to seek help from the most renowned ruler of the region, Dashrath, and had received the services of Ram and Lakshman.

The question is that Vishwamitra was a powerful sage-as much powerful as to threaten to create another set of creation[1].-yet he couldn't dare stop even the demon-lord, Ravan's 'border security force', headed by

1.It is held that camel against the original elephant; buffalo against the original cow were part of that attempt aborted mid way when his demands were met.

Khara, Dushan and Mareech. He knew that nothwithstanding his immense power he couldn't liquidate the demoniac supremacy growing every day. Another revered sage of that time, Vashishtha-the royal priest of Lord Ram's dynasty-the Solar dynasty-also was feeling helpless though he was reputed for having altered the order of time. There is an interesting story behind his this deed.

Long ago, after the creation had started functioning the Creator, Brahma, decided to land some of his chosen lieutenants on to the earth for ensuring its smooth functioning and growth of the righteous conduct among the beings. One of his chosen lieutenants was also Vashishtha, his psychic son. But Vashishtha resisted going to the earth with the plea : "here I am able to worship Lord Almighty undisturbed and there, on the earth, I would have to fight against so many distractions."

But the Creator said : "It's true but there you would have the chance of getting a vision of Lord Almighty Himself. He is committed to incarnate his image on the mortal plane whenever things go topsy-turvy there. And since decay is the natural tendency of the created things, his incarnating himself is a foregone conclusion. Then you would have a chance of seeing him personally."

"Is it true," asked exlilarated Vashishtha.

"When it is expected" he asked again.

"Now in Treta Yug will He incarnate with his maximum potency thus far". Brahma, the creator further added. "That would come as the Third Age[1], Treta."

Realising that he would have to wait for a full Yug (Age) he altered the order of the Ages by his yogic power and made Treta the second Age.

So, despite these sages being so immensely powerful they couldn't control or eliminate the demons. Hence both of them sort of urged Almighty for his Incarnation, for they had the power of communication with the Supreme spirit but no executive authority. If one studies the Ramayan with little independent reasoning one learns that it was sort of a divine conspiracy hatched by the sages which made Ram almost stand pitted against Ravain's authority. After his banishment from Ayodhya Ram always led the path directed by the sages-whether it be Bhardwaj sage or the sage Atri.

In Shankaracharya's case we see not only his deciding what ought to be done for the people but his doing it himself. Perhaps by that time God had decided to instinct humans with the divine spark instead of Himself coming down to the earth. Or, may be, the power of

[1] Treta by Sanskrit terminobogy is really the third age. If Satyayug was the first Age, Treta was to be the third Age and Dwapar by this very terminology the Second Age.

communication had gone weak. Whatever be the case, Shankaracharya had to set himself the order right in this part of the world. Being a precocious boy as he was, he had realised at a very tender age that the root cause of all ills was the people's misconstruing the sacred text. Some read only the letters with out realising the spirit and some stuck to the spirit without giving it an attractive form. With the result, there were the Karmakandis and the Gyanmargis and each group developing hostility for the other in the absence of total comprehension of the text. This made Shankaracharya polish the concept of Advaitism by asserting that both sects were right in their comprehension but that both were also complementary to each other in the true realisation. Although this might have been Shankaracharya's fundamental belief, he advocated for the supremacy of knowledge because he found that described form of that Ultimate knowledge was adding more of confusion than establishing clarity. Moreover, since most of the other faiths that had started affecting the psyche of the Indians pointed towards the formless Ultimate, it was even psychologically necessary for the retention of the perennial faith (Sanatam Dharam) that the formless Ultimate should be established as our own concept. That the concept existed from the very dawn of the civilisation cannot be denied. So he established his doctrine of Advaitism which not only strengthened the concept but also made people see the reason behind it.

To many people Shankaracharya's solidifying the cultural Unity might appear a far fetched idea. But why did he establish the four citadel of the faith-the Peethas at the four directional corners of the whole tract of our civilisation ? Moreover, why did he keep on travelling; for spreading his doctrine ? The answer to the last question is emphatic No ? He did all these things to clean the cobweb of ignorance setting over the ancient knowledge which itself was badly requiring revision. He travelled far and wide to tell people what they ought to do not by words but by deeds also. He was the only saint wedded to the ascetic order of highest degree but still cared for his worldly duties. How could one dare neglect one's mother and claim mother's superiority in his teachings.

In fact Shankaracharya was those rare enlightened souls who trod this mundane world for its spiritnal welfare and to tell it what is right and what is wrong, what is ephemenral and what is eternal and what is logical and what is whimsical. The celebrate Urdu poet Iqbal's this couplet fits well on this celebrated saint's life :

"Hazaaron saal Nargis[1] apnee benooree pe roti hai;
Badee mushkil se hota hai chaman me deeavar paida."
[For millennia the flower of Nargis wails over its sightlessness. It is very rarely that it blooms a flower having its own vision]

---

1. The narcissus flower. Normally its shape is like a closed eye and rarely blooms such a flower having an eye-like opening.

Book II

Shankaracharya' Selected works

[Their Original text, Romanised verson alongwith Hindi & English translations]

(१) द्वादश पंजरिका स्तोत्रम् [१]

मूढ जहीहि धनागमतृष्णां

कुरु सद्बुद्धिं मनसि वितृष्णाम्।

यल्लभसे निजकर्मोपात्तं वित्तं

तेन विनोदय चित्तम् ॥ १ ॥

भज गोविन्दं भज गोविन्दं गोविन्दं भज मूढमते॥ (ध्रुवपदम्)

ओ मूढ़! धनसंचय की लालसा छोड़, सुबुद्धि धारण कर, मन से तृष्णाहीन हो, अपने प्रारब्धानुसार तुझे जो कुछ वित्त मिल जाय, उसी से चित्त को प्रसन्न रख और हे मूढ़मते! निरंतम गोविन्दं भज! ॥ 1 ॥ (टेक)[2]

अर्थमनर्थं भावय नित्यं

नास्ति ततः सुखलेशः सत्यम्

पुत्रादपि धनभाजां भीतिः

सर्वत्रैषा विहिता नीतिः। भज० ॥ २॥

अर्थ को नित्य अनर्थरूप जान, उसमें सचमुच ही सुख का लेश भी नहीं है। अरे! सभी जगह ऐसी नीति देखी है कि धनवान को तो अपने पुत्र से भी भय रहता है—इसलिए सदा गोविन्दं भज ॥ २ ॥

का ते कान्ता कस्ते

पुत्रः संसारोऽयमतीव विचित्रः।

---

1. ऐसा माना जाता है कि यह स्त्रोत्र शंकराचार्य और उनके शिष्यों ने सम्मिलित रूप से सृजित किया था।

२. ध्रुवपद अर्थात, टेक जो हर पद के बाद दुहराई जाती है।

1 Twelve Commandments For the Disciples[1]

Moodha jaheehe dhanagaṁtrishna
kuru sadbuddhi manasi vitrishnam |
yallahhase nijakarmopattam vittam
tena vinodaya chittam|| 1 ||
Bhaj Govindam bhaj Govindam
bhaj Govindam moodha mate! (Burden)

O Fool ! Shed your passion for amassing wealth, be wise and make your mind devoid of craving. What ever money you get by your ordained fate be happy with that. And O tool ! ever Chant the name of Govinda || 1 || [Burden[2]]

Arthamanartham bhavaya nityam
nisti tatah sukhaleshah satyam!
Putredapi dhanbhajam bheetih
Sarvatreisha vihita neetih [Bhaj] || 2 ||

Deem wealth always as disturbance since that really lacks even an iota of happiness! The world is like that in which a rich man is afraid of even his own son. Hence the best course is your ever chanting the name of Govinda.

Ka te kanta kastey
Putrah Sansaroaya mateeva vichitrah!

[1] It is generally believed that these Strotras were composed collectively by Shankarcharya and his disciples.

[2] This line- 'ever chant the name of Govinda' is the burden of this composition.

कस्य त्वं कः कुत आयातस्तत्त्वं

चिन्तय यदिदं भ्रातः। भज० ॥ ३ ॥

कौन तेरी स्त्री है? कौन तेरा पुत्र? अरे! यह संसार बड़ा विचित्र है, भाई! इसी तत्त्व का निरंतर विचार कर कि 'तू कौन है? किसका है? और कहाँ से आया है?' और निरंतर गोविन्दं भज॥ ३॥

मा कुरु धनजनयौवनगर्वं

हरति निमेषात्कालः सर्वम्।

मायामयमिदमखिलं हित्वा

ब्रह्मपदं त्वं प्रविश विदित्वा। ॥ ४ ॥

धन, जन और यौवन का गर्व मत कर (चूँकि) काल पलक मारते ही इन सबको नष्ट कर देता है। इस संपूर्ण मायामय प्रपंच को छोड़ ब्रह्मपद को जान और उसी में प्रवेश कर! और हे मूढ़ सदा गोविन्द का भजन कर ॥ ४॥

काम क्रोधं लोभं मोहं

त्यक्त्वात्मानं भावय कोऽहम।

आत्मज्ञानविहीना मूढास्ते

पंज्यन्ते नरकनिगूढाः। भज० ॥ ५ ॥

काम, क्रोध, लोभ, मोह की त्याग कर अपने लिए विचार कर कि 'मैं कौन हूँ?' जो मूढ़ आत्मज्ञान से रहित हैं, वे नरक में पड़े हुए सन्तप्त होते रहते हैं! अतः सदा गोविन्दं को ही भज॥ ५॥

सुरमन्दिरतरुमूलनिवासः

शय्या भूतलमजिनं वासः।

Kasya tvam kah kuta

āyātastattvam chintaya yadiam bhratah ! Bhaj [3]

Who is your wife ? Who is your son ! Oh ! This world is really strange, ! Always brood over 'Who are you', where are you and wherefore have you come ?' And ever chant Govnida's, name || 3 ||

Ma kuru dhanajana yauvan garvam

harati nimeshāt kālah sarvam |

Māyā maya midamakhilam hitva

Brahmapadam tvam pravisha viditvā!

Never be proud of money, worldly benefits or youth since Time can distroy all of them in a trice ! Leave all these illusions, realise Supreme Being and surrender yourself unto Him ! And ever chant the name of Govnida || 4 ||

Kāmam krodham lobham Moham

tya ktvātmānam bhāvaya koham |

Atmagyānaviheena moodhāste

Pajyante naraka nigoodhah | Bhaj || 5 ||

Shed desire, anger, greed and infatuation and ever brood over: 'Who am I ?' The fools who are devoid of self-knowledge are as good as languishing in hell. Hence ever chant Govinda's name || 5 ||

Suramandir taru moola niwāsah

shaiyya bhootala majinam vāsah |

सर्वपरिग्रहभोगत्यागः

कस्य सुखं न करोति विरागः। भज० ॥ ६ ॥

देव मंदिर अथवा वृक्षातल का निवास, पृथ्वी की ही शैय्या, मृगचर्य का वस्त्र और सब प्रकार परिग्रह और भोगों का त्याग हो तो ऐसा वैराग्य किसको सुख नहीं पहुँचाता? अतः सदा गोविन्दं को भज॥ 6॥

शत्रौ मित्रे पुत्रे बन्धौ

मा कुरु यत्नं विग्रहसन्धौ।

भव समचित्तः सर्वत्र

त्वंञ्छस्यचिराद्यदि विष्णुत्वम्। ॥ ७ ॥

यदि तू शीघ्र विष्णुत्व की प्राप्ति का अभिलाषी है तो शत्रु, पुत्र और बन्धुओं से मेल अथवा अनमेल का प्रयास मत कर और सर्वत्र सम भाव रखते हुए निरंतर गोविन्दं का भजन कर॥ 7॥

त्वयि मयि चान्यत्रैको

विष्णुर्व्यर्थं कुप्यसि सर्वसहिष्णुः।

सर्वस्मिन्नपि पश्यात्मानं

सर्वत्रोत्सृज भेदाज्ञानम्। भज० ॥ ८ ॥

तुझमें, मुझमें और अन्यत्र भी सब में एक ही वासुदेव हैं इसलिए कोप करना व्यर्थ है। सब को सहन करने वाला होकर आत्मा (ईश्वर-अंश) को ही सबमें विद्यमान देख; भेद रूपी अंधकार का त्याग कर दे और सर्वदा 'गोविन्दं' का भजन कर॥ 8॥

Sarvaparigrihabhogatyāgah

kasya sukham na karoti virāgah | Bhaj || 6 ||

Dwelling in the temples or at the base of a tree and sleeping ever on hard earth; wearing only deer-skin and shunning all kinds of plesures and possessions whom such detachment won't give bliss? Hence ever chant Govida's name || 6 ||

Shatrau mitre putre bandhau

ma kuru yathnam vigrahasandhau |

Bhava sam chittah sarvartra

tvamchhasyachiradyādi Vishnutvam | Bhaj || 7 ||

It you earnestly desire attaining to Lord Vishnu's realm, don't try to get close to your kiths and friends and be away from your enemies or opponents. Be equinamous with all and ever chant Govinda's name || 7 ||

Tvayi mayi chanya treiko

Vishuvyartham kupyasi sarvasahishnuh |

Sarvasi mannapi pashyatmanam

sarvatrotsraj bhedagyānam| Bhaj || 8 ||

For the same Lord Vasudva dwells in you and me and in everything in this universe. Hence it is futile to he angry with any one as all are instinct with the same Spirit. Be tolerant and view that Divine Spirit present in every one. Shed your ignorance that makes you see the differecnes, and ever chant the name of Govnida || 8 ||

प्राणायामं प्रत्याहारं

नित्यानित्यविवेकविचारम्।

जाप्यसमेतसमाधिविधानं

कुर्ववधानं महदवधानम्। भज० ॥ ९ ॥

प्राणायाम, प्रत्याहार और नित्या नित्य वस्तु का विवेक पूर्वक विचार कर, विधि-पूर्वक भगवन्नामस्मरण के सहित ध्यान करने का निश्चय कर-क्योंकि यही महान निश्चय है, और सदा गोविन्दं का भजन कर॥ 9 ॥

नलिनीदलगतसलिलं तरलं

तद्वज्जीवितमतिशय चपलम्।

विद्धि व्याध्यभिमानग्रस्तं लोकं

शोकहतं च समस्तम्। भज० ॥ १० ॥

कमल पत्र पर पड़ी हुई जैसे जल की बूँद स्थिर नहीं होती वैसा ही अति चंचल यह जीवन है; इसे खूब समझ ले! व्याधि और अभिमान से ग्रस्त हुआ यह सारा संसार अति शोकाकुल है—अतः तू सदा गोविन्दं को भज॥ 10 ॥

का तेऽष्टादशदेशे चिन्ता वातुल

तव किं नास्ति नियन्ता।

यस्त्वां हस्ते सुदृढनिबद्धं बोधयति

प्रभवादिविरुद्धम्। भज० ॥ ११ ॥

रे पागल जीव! तू अठाहर जगह की चिन्ता क्यों कर रहा है, क्या तेरा कोई नियन्ता नहीं है? जो तेरे दोनों हाथ बाँधकर तुझे जन्म-मरणादि

Pranāyāmam Pratyāhāram

nityānitya viveka vichāram |

Japyasametasamādhi vidhānan

kurvavadhānam mahadavadhanām | Bhaj || 9 ||

Exercising breath-control, with drawing the senses from external objects and discerning what is eternal and what is transistory, make resolve of religiously worshipping lord Almighty because this is the solc true determination in the mortal world. Ever chant Govinda's name || 9 ||

Nalinidalagatasalilam taralan-

tadvat jjivita matishaya chapalam |

Viddhi vyadhyabhimanagrastam lokam

shokahatam cha samastam | Bhaj || 10 ||

This life is ever unstable like the drop of water lying on the petal of lotus-realise this comprehensively ! This whole world is distressed with the menace of 'I-Ness' and a variety of diseases. Hence your welfare lies in ever chanting the name of Govinda

Ka teashtadashdeshe chinta vatul

tav kim nāsti niyanta |

Yastvām haste sudrirhanibaddham bodhayati

prabhavādiviruddham | Bhaj || 11 ||

O Ye insane being ! Why must you worry, for what is happening at umpteen places ? Do you think there is no one to regulate life in the world? Do you want Him to bind you into inactivity so that you may realise what

विकारों से रहित आत्मतत्व का बोध करा सके ? अरे मूढ़ ! सर्वदा गोविन्दं का भजन कर ॥ 11 ॥

गुरुचरणाम्बुजनिर्भरभक्तः

संसारादचिराभ्दव मुक्तः

सेन्द्रियमानसनियमादेवं द्रक्ष्यसि

निजहृदयस्थं देवम् । भज० ॥ १२ ॥

द्वादशपञ्चरिकामय एषः शिष्याणां

कथितो ह्युपदेशः ।

येषां चित्ते नैव विवेकस्ते पच्यन्ते

नरकमनेकम् । भज० ॥ १३ ॥

इति श्रीमच्डङ्कराचार्यरिचितं द्वादशापञ्चरिकास्तोत्रं सम्पूर्णम् ।

गुरुदेव के चरण कमलों का अनन्य भक्त होकर संसार से तू शीघ्र मुक्त हो जा ! इस प्रकार इन्द्रियों के सहित मन का संयम करने से तू शीघ्र ही अपने हृदयस्थ देव को देखेगा, अत: निरंतर गोविन्दं का भजन कर ॥ 12 ॥ यह द्वादश पंजारिका स्तोत्र शिष्यों के उपदेश के लिए कहा गया है । जिनके हृदय में विवेक नही है वे दीर्घ काल तक नरक यातना भोगते हैं ! अत: हे मूढ़ मते ! तू निरंतर गोविन्दं का भजन कर ॥ 3 ॥

[इस प्रकार श्रीमद् शंकराचार्य द्वारा 'द्वादश पंजारिका स्तोत्र' सम्पूर्ण हुआ]

actually you are ? fool ? Ever chant the name of Govinda || 11 ||

Gurucharanāmbuja nirbhar bhaktah
sansaradachiradbhva muktah!
Sendriyamānasniyamā devam drakshyasi
nijahridayastham devam | Bhaj || 12 ||
Dwādashapanjarikamaya eshah shishyānam
kathito hyupdcshah |
Yesham chitte naiva vivekastey pachyantey
narkamanekam | Bhaj || 13 ||

Be a dedicated dcvotee to your guru's lotus-like feet and liberate yourself from the world soon ! Thus with- drawing all your senses from external objects and concentrating them unto your internal self you will soon see the Divine spirit reposing on your heart. Hence always keep on chanting the name of Govinda. For those who lack this discernment ever languish in hell suffer ing all kinds of tortures. Hence o fool ! chant ever the name of Govinda || 13 ||

[This completes Dwādashpanjanika Strotra' created by Shankaracharya].

कौपीनपञ्चकं स्तोत्रम्[1]

वेदान्तवाक्येषु सदा रमन्तो भिक्षान्नमात्रेण च तुष्टिमन्तः।
अशोकवन्तः करुणैकवन्तः कौपीनवन्तः खलु भाग्यवन्तः॥ १॥

मूलं तरोः केवलमाश्रयन्तः पाणिद्वये भोक्तुममत्रयन्तः।
कन्थामपि स्त्रीमिव कुत्सयन्तः कौपीनवन्तः खलु भाग्यवन्तः॥ २॥

देहाभिमानं परिहृत्य दूरादात्मानमात्मन्यवलोकायन्तः।
अहर्निशं ब्रह्मणि ये रमन्तः कौपीनवन्तः खलु भाग्यवन्तः॥ ३॥

स्वानन्दभावे परितुष्टिमन्तः स्वशान्तसर्वोन्द्रियवृत्तिमन्तः।
नान्तं न मध्यं न बहिः स्मरन्तः कौपीनवन्तः खलु भाग्यवन्तः॥ ४॥

पञ्चाक्षरं पावनमुच्चरन्तः पतिं पशूनां हृदि भावयन्तः।
भिक्षाशना दिक्षु परिभ्रमन्तः कौपीनवन्तः खलु भाग्यवन्तः॥ ५॥

---

1. शंकराचार्य की यह तीन कृतियाँ : 'द्वादश पंजरिका स्तोत्रम, को पीन पंचकम् स्त्रोत्रम' और इस पुस्तक के अन्त में दिया हुआ 'चर्पटपंजरिका स्तोत्रम' अति प्रसिद्ध और बहु उद्धरित रचनाएं हैं। इनके द्वारा शंकराचार्य ने क्रमशः विद्यार्थियों या बटुकों, साधू-संन्यासियों तथा गृहस्थों को सही प्रकार से जीवन यापन का उपदेश दिया है और इस प्रकार मानव जीवन की सम्पूर्ण अवस्थाओं में आदर्श जीवन किस प्रकार बिताया जाय, यह बताया है।

Commandments For The Hermits[1]

Vedāntavakyeshu sadā ramanto bhikshannāmatrenacha tushtimantah |

Ashokavantah karuneikavantah kaupeenavantah khalu bhāgyavantah || 1 ||

Moolam taroh kevalamāshryantah paninadvaye bhotumamatrayantah |

Kanthamapi streemiva kutsayantah kaupeenavantah khalu bhāgyaavantah || 2 ||

Dehabhimanam parihritya dooradātmāna mātmanyavalokayantah |

Aharnisham Brahmani ye ramantah kaupeenvantah khalu bhāgyavantah || 3 ||

Swānandabhāve paritushtamantah Swashāntasarvondriyavrithimantah

Nantam na madhyam na bahih smaramtah kaupeenavantah khalu bhagyavantah || 4 ||

Panchaksharam pavanamuchcharantah patim pashoonām hridi bhavantah |

Bhikshashana dikshu paribhramantah kaupeenvantah khalu bhāgyavantah || 5 ||

---

1. These three compostion viz : 'Dwadeshpanjarika Stotram', this 'Kaupeena panchak Strotram' and the one given in the end of this book, 'Charpatapanjarika Strotram' are Shakaracharya's oft-quoted and famous creations. While the first one is meant of the young ones or the students, this one for the hermits or ascetics and the last one is mainly addresed to the men with family. This way the erudite-sage has tried to cover the whole span of human life and shown each of them the ideal way of leading their life in their respective stages.

सदैव उपनिषद द्वारा प्राप्त किए हुए वाक्यों में रमते हुए (अर्थात् सदैव उनका मनन और उन पर चिंतन करते हुए), भिक्षा के अन्न मात्र में ही संतोष रखते हुए (अर्थात् भिक्षा में जो अन्न मिल जाए उसी से पूर्णतया संतुष्ट हो आहार ग्रहण करते हुए) शोक रहित तथा दयावान, कौपीन धारण करने वाले ही भाग्यवान हैं ॥ 1 ॥

केवल वृक्षतलों में (अर्थात् पेड़ों के नीचे) रहने वाले, दोनों हाथों को ही भोजन पात्र बनाने वाले, गुदड़ी को स्त्री की भाँति तुच्छ बुद्धि से देखने वाले (अर्थात् स्त्री के प्रति कोई आकर्षण न रखने वाले—बल्कि उनके प्रति एक तरह तिरस्कार भाव ही रखने वाले) कौपीन धारी ही भाग्यवान हैं ॥ 2 ॥

देहाभिमान को दूर से ही छोड़कर, अपनी आत्मा को अपने में ही देखते हुए रात-दिन ब्रह्म में भ्रमण करने वाले कौपीन धारी ही भाग्यवान हैं। (अर्थात् आदर्श संन्यासी वही है जो देह संबंधी अभिमानों के परे रहते हुए आत्मा को ब्रह्म के अंश के रूप में देखता है और उसका ध्यान सदैव ब्रह्म या सर्वशक्ति सत्ता-ईश्वर-के प्रति केन्द्रित रहता है। वही संन्यासी भाग्यवान है जो ऐसा कर सके ॥ 3 ॥)

आत्मानंद में ही संतुष्ट रहने वाले, अपने भीतर ही सारी इन्द्रियों की वृत्तियाँ शांत कर लेने वाले, अन्त मध्य और बाहर की स्मृति से शून्य

Ever contemplating upon the pithy observation made by the Upanishads ; feeling totally satisfied with food received as alms (i.e. without cribbing about the food's taste and favour and consuming it with apparent satisfaction) ; free from any streak of sorrow for, one only sorrows for someone only due to emotional attachment and a true saunyasi ought to be beyond any personal prejudices or predilections since the person observing the vows of this highest order has to view this the world animate and inanimati-with one single vision ; having emapathy for all with even compassion are the characterstics of the fortunate Kaupeendharis[1] || 1 ||

Those Kaupeendharis are fortunate who ever dwell beneath the trees; whose utensils for having food are their two hands; who look at a bundle of clothes and a woman with same-feeling (i.e. those who have no attraction for woman and, on the contrary, they have contempt for any such attractions) and donot differentiate between them || 2 ||

Fortunate are those Kaupeendharis who ever remain in constant communion with the self or Supreme Being and ever cngrossed in the bliss of self. || 3 ||

Fortumate are those Kanpeendharis who appear ever content with the blises of self who have totally snappped their senses proclivity towards external objects and who have their minds like

1. Literally a tiny of cloth to barely cover the privities. Allegorically it means those Sanyasis who wear it to symbolise their total detachmerer from the world.

रहने वाले कौपीन धारी ही भाग्यवान हैं ॥ 4 ॥ (अर्थात् संन्यासी को बाहरी जगत से अप्रभावित रहना चाहिए।) उसे अपने आत्मानंद में ही लीन रहना चाहिए और समग्र इन्द्रियों को बाहरी आकर्षणों के प्रति विमुख कर भीतर-ही-भीतर उनकी सहज बहिर्मुखी होने की प्रवृत्ति का शमन कर लेना चाहिए। यदि संन्यासी को अपने पूर्व काल की स्मृति रहेगी तो उसकी इन्द्रियों पर पूरा नियंत्रण नहीं रहेगा। यहाँ शंकराचार्य का तात्पर्य इन्द्रियों की वृत्तियों का शमन करने से, न कि उनका मात्र दमन करने का–क्योंकि दमन उनकी बहिर्मुखी प्रवृत्तियों को और उभारेगा। यह प्रकृति का नियम है कि दबाई हुई प्रवृत्ति की स्वतः चेष्टा विपरीत दिशा में ही प्रस्फुटन की होती है, जबकि शमन का अर्थ है उस प्रवृत्ति को पूर्णतः शांत करना, उसके अस्तित्व को ही तिरोहित करना है।)

पवित्र पंचमाक्षर मंत्र ('नमः शिवाय') का जाप करते हुए, हृदय में परमेश्वर की भावना का संचार करते हुए (अर्थात् परमेश्वर का अनवरत स्तवन करते हुए); भिक्षा द्वारा प्राप्त भोजन को पूर्ण संतुष्टि से ग्रहण करते हुए और सब दिशाओं में विचरने वाले कौपीन धारी भाग्यवान् हैं।

(यहाँ ध्यान देने की बात यह है कि कौपीन धारी अर्थात् संन्यासी को एक स्थान पर टिक कर नहीं रहना चाहिए वरन् सर्वत्र विचरण करना चाहिए—क्योंकि एक जगह लगातार रहने से उस स्थान के प्रति मोह जागृत हो सकता है।)

'tabula rasa' sans any shades of either memory of the past of the consciousness of the present || 4 ||

Ever chanting the Five syllabled mantra (OM NAMAH SHIVAYA) and Concentrating on God ; deriving satisfaction from food received as alms and ever roaming about are those Kaupeendharis who are fortunate (or real), || 5 ||

(It may be noticed that Shankaracharya prohibits the ascetic of the highest order to stay at a particular place for long because, as is natural, prolonged stay might engender infatuation or affection with that place.

3. परापूजा

अखण्डे सच्चिदानंदे निर्विकल्पैकरूपिणि।
स्थितेऽद्वितीयभावेऽस्मिन्कथं पूजा विधीयते॥ १॥

पूर्वस्यावाहनं कुत्र सर्वाधारस्य चासनम्।
स्वच्छस्य पाद्यमर्घ्यं च शुद्धस्याचमनं कुतः॥ २॥

निर्मलस्य कुतः स्नानं वस्त्रं विश्वोदरस्य च।
अगोत्रस्य त्ववर्णस्य कुतस्तस्योपवीतकम्॥ ३॥

निर्लेपस्य कुतो गन्धः पुष्पं निर्वासनस्य च।
निर्विशेषस्य का भूषा कोऽलङ्कारो निराकृतेः॥ ४॥

निरञ्जनस्य किं धूपैर्दीपैर्वा सर्वसाक्षिणः।
निजानन्दैकतृप्तस्य नैवेद्यं किं भवेदिह॥ ५॥

अखंड, सच्चिदानन्द और निर्विकल्पैकरूप अद्वितीय भाव के स्थिर हो जाने पर, किस प्रकार पूजा की जाय?॥ 1॥

जो पूर्ण है उसका आह्वान कहाँ किया जाय? जो सबका आधार है उसे आसन किस वस्तु का दें? जो स्वच्छ है उसको पाद्य (पाद्‌य) कैसे दें? जो नित्य शुद्ध है उसको आचमन की क्या अपेक्षा?॥ 2॥

Transcendental worship

Akhande sacchidānande nirvikalpeirakaroopini |
Sthiteadwateeyabhāveasminkathatam poojā vidheeyate || 1 ||

Pooruāsyavāhanam kutra sarvadharāsya chasanam |
Swachchhasya pādyamarghyam cha shuddhasya chamanām kutah || 1 ||

Nirmalasya kutah snanam vastram vishwodarasya cha|
Agotrasya twavavarnasya kutastasyopaveetakam || 3 ||

Nirlepasya kuto gandhah pushpam nirvasanrya cha|
Nirvisheshasya ka bhoosha koalankaro nirākriteh|
Niranjanasya kim dhoopeirdeepeirva sarvasakshanah|
Nijānandeiktriptasya neivedyam kim bhavedih || 5 ||

How to worship him who is indefinable, the beacon of all that is good, beautiful and blissful reposing in his unique manner in his Insupplantable One and only Form ? || 1 ||

Where to invoke him who is complete and all pervading ? How to offer him any seat who is the base of entire creaton? How to offer him any ablution who is pious and blemishless and why should he need any cleansing operations who is absolutely pure? || 2 ||

निर्मल को स्नान कैसा? सम्पूर्ण विश्व जिसके उदर में है उसे वस्त्र कैसा? (अर्थात् उसे कौन देख सकता है?) जो वर्ण और गोत्र से रहित है उसके लिए यज्ञोपवीत कैसा?॥ 3॥

निर्लेप को गन्ध कैसी? निर्वासनिक थी पुष्पों से क्या? निर्विशेष को शोभा की क्या अपेक्षा और निराकार के लिए आभूषण क्या? निरंजन को धूप से क्या? सर्वसाक्षी को दीप कैसा तथा जो निजानन्द रूप अमृत से तृप्त है उसे नैवेद्य क्या?

(शंकराचार्य ने इन श्लोकों द्वारा ईश्वर की चरमता, पूर्णता और सर्वसम्पन्नता की ओर इंगित किया है? ईश्वर के अन्य अंशों की विभिन्न वस्तुओं से आराधना की जाती है पर स्वयं परमात्मा को, जो अद्वितीय है, अखंड है, असीम है, इन सब वस्तुओं की क्या आवश्यकता हो सकती है)

विश्वानन्दपितुस्तस्य किं ताम्बूलं प्रकल्प्यते |
स्वयंप्रकाशचिद्रूपो योऽसावर्कादिभासकः || ६ ||
प्रदक्षिणा ह्यनन्तस्य ह्यद्वयस्य कुतो नतिः |
वेदवाक्यैरवेद्यस्य कुतः स्तोत्रं विधीयते || ७ ||
स्वयंप्रकाशमानस्य कुतो नीराजनं विभोः |
अन्तर्बहिश्च पूर्णस्य कथमुद्वासनं भवेत् || ८ ||
एवमेव परापूजा सर्वावस्थासु सर्वदा |
एकबुद्धया तु देवेशे विधेया ब्रह्मवित्तमैः || ९ ||
आत्मा त्वं गिरिजा मतिः सहचराः प्राणाः शरीरं गृहं
पूजा ते विविधोपभोगरचना निद्रा समाधिस्थितिः |

Why must the unsullied need to bathe ? Why should he clad himself who has enter universe inside his belly. [i.e. who can see whether he is clad or not ?]. Of what significance is the sacred thread to Whom beyond Castes and Categaries reckoning

Why must he need any perfume who is detached from everyone. Why must he have a any significance of flowers who is an Eremite ? Why should some-one common to all need any especial decoration ? Who does the formless need adornment ? What is sun shine to the Omniscient ? Of what purpose is a lamp is to the one seeing every thing? And should he, fully content need any oblation.?

Vishwananda pitustasya kim tamboolam prakalpyate?
Swayamprakāsha chidroopo yoasāvarkardi bhasakah ||6||
Pradakshina hyanatasya hriyadvayasya kuto natih: !
Vedavākyaeiravedyasya kutah stotram vidheeyate ||7||
Swayamprakashamā-nasya kuto neerājanan vibhoh!
Antarbahishcha poornasya kathamudwāsanam bhavet ||8||
Evameva parapuja saravasthasu sarvada!
Ekabudhya tu deveshe vidheyā brahmvittameih ||9||
Atmā twam Girija matih sahacharāh prānāh shareeram griham
Pooja te vividhopabhogarachanā nidra samādhi sthitih

सञ्चारः पदयोः प्रदक्षिणाविधिः स्तोत्राणि सर्वा गिरो
यद्यत्कर्म करोमि तत्तदखिलं शम्भो तवाराधनम् || १० ||
इति श्रीमच्छङ्कराचार्यकृतं परापूजास्तोत्रं सम्पूर्णम् |

जो स्वयंप्रकाश, चित्स्वरूप, सूर्य चन्द्रादि का भी अवभासक और विश्व को आनन्दित करने वाला है, उसे क्या ताम्बूल समर्पण किया जाय ||६||

[ताम्बूल या पान किसी को भेंट करना उसकी महत्ता को स्वीकार करना है परन्तु जो संसार का स्वामी है उसे क्या ताम्बूल दिया जाय-वह तो है ही सबसे महान (यहाँ ध्यान देने योग्य तथ्य है कि यह सब वस्तुएं पूजा में समर्पण की जाती हैं परन्तु शंकराचार्य के मतानुसार ईश्वर को इनकी आवश्यकता ही नहीं है] अनन्त की परिक्रमा कैसी? अद्वितीय को नमस्कार कैसा ? ||७|| और जो वेदों के स्तवन द्वारा भी जाना न जा सके उसका स्तवन कैसे किया जाय ? जो बाहर भीतर सब ओर से परिपूर्ण है उसका विसर्जन कैसे हो ? ||८|| ब्रह्मवेत्ताओं को सर्वदा, सब अवस्थाओं में इसी प्रकार की बुद्धि से भगवान की परापूजा करनी चाहिए ||९|| हे शम्भो! मेरी आत्मा ही तुम हो, बुद्धि श्री पार्वती जी हैं, प्राण आपके गण हैं, शरीर आपकी कुटिया है नाना प्रकार की भोग सामग्री आपका पूजोपचार है; निद्रा समाधि है, मेरा चरणों पर चलना आपकी प्रदक्षिणा है और जो भी कुछ मैं बोलता हूँ वह सब आपके स्तोत्र हैं! अधिक क्या (कहूँ), मैं जो कुछ भी करता हूँ वह सब आपकी आराधाना ही है ||१०||

Sancharah padyoh pradakshinavidhih strotrani sarva giro Yadyatakarm karomi tattdakhilam · Shambho tavaradhanam ||10||
{ This completes Shankaracharya created parapoojastrotram}

How to offer the (honorific) betel leaf to him who is self-glowing of all consciousness, the light that radiates from the sun and the moon and makes them seen; the ultimate source of bliss to the entire world. [offering betel leaves and other sacred-things to deities is a customeay practice but through these Shlokas Shankaracharya has emphasised the futility of these offerings to Almighty who is complete, consummate and satiate in all respects] How to bow before one who is unique and ever present everywhere?. He who couldn't be assessed by all Vedas and Scriptuers is beyond the reach of any hymn. How to move lighted lamps around him who is the source of all light?. He who is consummate internally, externally and in every way can't be discarded either.||6-8||

All those who are versed in the ultimate knowledge of Brahman (Supreme Being) should worship Almighty through this kind of transcendental worship. Lord shankar (Shiv)-You are by soul; goddess Parvati my wisdom; my life-breath represents your attendants; my body is your hermitage; my food is your oblation; my sleep is your samadhi; my movement is moving around you from the right side and whatever I do is your worship [That is the devotee is totally represented by his Lord.]

4. चर्पट पंजरिका स्तोत्रम्

दिनमपि रजनी सायं प्रातः शिशिरवसन्तौ पुनरायातः

कालः क्रीडति गच्छत्यायुस्तदपि न मुञ्चतशावायुः

भज गोविन्दं भज गोविन्दं भज गोविन्दं मूढमते।

प्राप्ते सन्निहते मरणे नहि नहि रक्षति डुकृञ्करणे। (ध्रुवपदम्)

अग्रे वह्निः पृष्ठे भानू रात्रौ चिबुकसमर्पितजानु।

करतलभिक्षा तरुतलवासस्तदपि न मुन्यत्याशापाशः। भज० ||२||

दिन और रात, सायंकाल और प्रातःकाल, शिशिर और वसन्त पुनः पुनः आते हैं, इसी प्रकार काल की लीला होती है और आयु बीत जाती है—किन्तु आशारूपी वायु छोड़ती ही नहीं; अतः हे मूढ़ ! निरन्तर गोविन्द को ही भज क्योंकि मृत्यु के समीप आने पर 'डुकृञ् करणे' की रटना रक्षा नहीं कर सकेगी || 1 ||

दिन में आगे अग्नि और पीछे सूर्य तपाते हैं, रात्रि के समय जानुओं में ठोड़ी दबाए पड़े रहते हैं; हाथ में ही भिक्षा माँग लाते हैं, वृक्ष के तले ही पड़े रहते हैं—फिर भी आशा का जाल जकड़े रहता है ! अतः हे मूढ़—गोविन्द को ही भज .... इत्यादि

Commandments for Men with Family

Dinamapi Rajani s̄ayam pr̄atah shishiravasantau punarayatah |

Kalah kreedati gachchhatyayustadapi na munchaty̆āshāvayuh || 1 ||

Bhaja Govindam bhaja Govindam bhaja Govindam moodhamate |

Prapte sannihitey marane nahi nahi rakshati 'Dukrih karane'[1] ||

Agne vahinha prishthe bhānoo ratrau chibukasamarkitajanuh ||

Kartal bhiksha tar̄utalavasastadapi na m̄unchatya ashapashah | Bhaja || 2 ||

Time maintains its cycle with the day following the night; autumn following spring and this way age gets over but hope never leaves one's life-breath ! Worship Govinda, o fool ! How will the rules of grammar help you when death is nigh ! || 1 ||

While in day fire singes from front and the sun from behind and during the night pressing our kness against the chin we lie ; begging edibles as alms and carrying them in the cavity formed by joining hands we idle away our time beneath a tree yet the clutches of hope keep us in their hold. Hence, o fool, worship Govinda ! How will the rules of grammar help you when death is nigh ! || 2 ||

1. A rule of Sanskrit Grammar. Seeing an oldman chanting this rule to cram it, Shankarcharya instructed him this way.

यावद्वित्तोपार्जनसक्तस्तावन्निजपरिवारो रक्तः।

पश्चाज्जीवति जर्जरदेहे वार्तां पृच्छति कोऽपि न गेहे। भज० ॥ ३ ॥

जटिलो मुण्डी लुञ्चितकेशः काषायाम्बरबहुकृतवेषः।

पश्यन्नपि च न पश्यति लोको ह्युदरनिमित्तं बहुकृतशोकः।

भज० ॥ ४ ॥

भगवद्गीता किञ्चिदधीता गङ्गाजललवकणिकापीता।

सकृदपि यस्य मुरारिसमर्चा तस्य यमः किं कुरुते चर्चाम।

भज० ॥ ५ ॥

अङ्गं गलितं पलितं मुण्डं दशनविहीनं जातं तुण्डम्।

वृद्धो याति गृहीत्वा दण्डं तदपि न मुञ्चत्याशा पिण्डम्। ॥ ६ ॥

अरे, जब तक तू धन कमाने में लगा हुआ है तभी तक तेरा परिवार तुझ से प्रेम करता है। जब जरा ग्रस्त होगा तब कोई घर में बात भी न पूछेगा ; अतः हे मूढ़ निरंतर गोविन्द को ही भज, क्योंकि मृत्यु के समीप आने पर 'डुकृञ् करणे'-यह रटना रक्षा न कर सकेगी ॥ ३ ॥

जटाजूट धारी हो कर, मुण्डित होकर, लुचित केश होकर, काषायाम्बरधारी होकर, ऐसे नाना प्रकार के वेष धारण करके यह मनुष्य देखता हुआ भी नहीं देखता और पेट के लिए नाना प्रकार से शोक किया करता है! अतः हे मूढ़! निरंतर-गोविन्द को ही भज ॥ ४ ॥

जिसने भगवतद्गीता को कुछ भी पढ़ा है, गंगाजल की एक बूंद भी पी है, एक बार भी जिसने भगवान् कृष्ण की अर्चना की है उसकी यमराज क्या चर्चा कर सकता है ? अतः हे मूढ़!

Yāvadwittopārjansaktstā vannijaparivāro raktah |

Pashchāddhā jarjar- dehe vārtān prichchhati koapi na gehe| Bhaja || 3 ||

Jatilo mundee lunchitakeshaha kashayambarab ahukritaveshah |

Pashyannapi cha na pashyati loko hyudaranimittam bahukritashokah | Bhaja || 4 ||

Bhagwatgeeta kinchidadheetā Gangājalalavakanikapeetā

Sakridapi yasya murarisamarcha tasya yamah kim kurute chercham | Bhaja || 5 ||

Angam galitam palitam mundam dashanaviheenam jatam tundam |

Vriddho yati griheetvaa dandam tadapi munchatyasha pindam | Bhaja || 6 ||

Listen ! Till you are engrossed in amassing wealth your family loves you. When you become old and weak no one in your house would even enquire about you ! Hence, O fool ! Worship Govinda ! How will the rules of grammar help you when death is nigh || 3 ||

Even by changing his appearance repeatedly-now having long locks, unkempt and growing wildly and now having a clean shaven hair or having his hair plucked even-man doesn't see the obvious and troubles himself in a variety of ways-grieving and fretting-for earning his bread ! Hence O Fool ! Worship Govnida ! How will the rules of grammar help you when death is nigh || 4 ||

He who has even fractionally read the Srimad bhagwat Geeta' ; partaken even a drop of the Ganga water or even

बालस्तावत्क्रीडासक्तस्तरुणस्तावत्तरुणीरक्तः।
वृद्धस्तावच्चिन्तामग्नः पारे ब्रह्मणि कोऽपि न लग्नः । भज० ॥ ७॥

पुनरपि जननं पुनरपि मरणं पुनरपि जननीजठरे शयनम्।
इह संसारे खलु दुस्तारे कृपयापारे पाहि मुरारे। भज० ॥ ८ ॥

पुनरपि रजनी पुनरपि दिवसः पुनरपि पक्षः पुनरपि मासः।
पुनरप्ययनं पुनरपि वर्षं तदपि न मुंचत्याशामर्षम्। भज० ॥ ९ ॥

वयसि गते कः कामविकारः शुष्के नीरे कः कासारः।
नष्टे द्रव्ये कः परिवारो ज्ञाते तत्त्वे कः संसारः। भज० ॥ १० ॥

निरंतर गोविन्द को ही भज, क्योंकि मृत्यु के समीप आने पर 'डुकृञ् करणे' की रटना रक्षा न कर सकेगी ॥ 5 ॥

अंग गलित हो गए, सिर के बाल पक गये, मुख के दाँत नहीं रहे, बूढ़ा हो गया, लाठी लेकर चलने लगा, फिर भी आशा पिण्ड नहीं छोड़ती, अतः हे मूढ़ ! निरंतर गोविन्द को ही भज, क्योंकि मृत्यु के समीप आने पर 'डकृञ् करणे' कर रटना रक्षा न कर सकेगी ॥ 6 ॥

बालक तो खेल-कूद में आसक्त रहता है, तरुण स्त्री में आसक्त रहता है और वृद्ध भी नाना प्रकार की चिन्ताओं में मग्न रहता है, पर ब्रह्म में कोई संलग्न नहीं होता, अतः अरे मूढ़ ! तू सदा गोविन्द का ही भजन

Balastavatkreedasakratastarunastavattarune eraktah|

Vriddhastavachchintamagnah pare brahmani koapi na lagnah | Bhaja || 7 ||

Punarapi jananam punarapi maranam punarapi jananijathare shayanam

Iha sansare khalu dustare kripayapare pahi Murāre | Bhaja || 8 ||

Punarapi rajani punarapi diwasah punarapi pakshah punarapi māsah |

Punarapyayanam punarapi varsham tadapi na munchtyāsha marsham | Bhaja || 9 ||

Vayasigate kah kamvikarah shushke neere kah kāsorah |

Nashte dravye kah parivaro gyate tatve kah sansarah | Bhaja || 10 ||

once worshipped lord Krishna is beyord the reach of the death god (Yamraj) ! Hence O fool ! Worship Govinda, How will the rules of grammar help you when death is nigh || 5 ||

Even when body limbs grow weak, hair turn grey, teeth are lost in the mouth ; one has grown too old and unassisted as much as to walk with the support of a stick, hope never leaves one ! Hence O fool ! Worship Govinda because when death is nigh the rules of grammar won't be able to protect you. || 6 ||

Lost is the child in play ; in his beloved's charm. the youth ; the aged are lost in their worries and

नारीस्तनभरनाभिनिवेशं मिथ्यामायामोहावेशम्।
एतन्मांसवसादिविकारं मनसि विचारय बारम्बारम्। भज० ॥ ११ ॥

कस्त्वं कोऽहं कुत आयातः का मे जननी को मे तातः।
इति परिभावय सर्वमसारं विश्वं त्यक्त्वा स्वप्रविचारम्।
भज० ॥१२॥

गेयं गीतानामसहस्त्रं ध्येयं श्रीपतिरूपमजस्त्रम्।
नेयं सज्जनसङ्गे चित्तं देयं दीनजनाय च वित्तम्। भज० ॥ १३ ॥

यावज्जीवो निवसति देहे कुशलं तावत्पृच्छति गेहे।
गतवति वायौ देहापाये भार्या बिभ्यति तस्मिन्काये। भज० ॥ १४ ॥

सुखतः क्रियते रामाभोगः पश्चद्धन्त शरीरे रोगः।
यद्यपि लोके मरणं शरणं तदपि न मुञ्चचि
पापाचरणम्। भज० ॥ १५ ॥

रथ्याचर्पटविरचितकन्थः पुण्यापुण्यविवर्जितपन्थः।
नाहं न त्वं नायं लोकस्तदपि किमर्थं क्रियते शोकः।भज० ॥ १६ ॥

कुरुते गङ्गासागरगमनं व्रतपरिपालनमथवा दामन्।
ज्ञानविहीनः सर्वमतेन मुक्तिं न भजति जन्मशतेन। भज० ॥ १७ ॥

Nareestanabhārnabhinivcsham mithyāmāyāmo hāvesham

Etanmāsnavasadivikāram manasi vicharaya bārambāram | Bhaja || 11 ||

Kastvam koaham kuta āyātah ka me janani ko me tātah |

Iti paribhavāya sarvamsāram vishwamtyaktva swapna vichāram || 12 ||

Geyam Geetānāmasahastram dhyeyam shreepatiroopamajastram |

Neyam sajjansange chittam deyam deenajanāya cha vittam | Bhaja || 13 ||

Yavajjewo nivasati dehe kushalam tavataprichchati gehe |

Gativati vayau dehapaye bhārya bibhyati tasminkāye | Bhaja

Sukhatah kriyati rāmabhogah paschadhanta shareere rogah |

Yadyapi loke maranam shararam tadapi na munchati pāpacharanam | Bhaje

Rathyācharpatavirachitakanthah punyāpunyaviva rjitapanthah |

Naham na tvam nayam lokastadapi kimartham kriyati shokah | Bhaja

Kuruta Gangāsagaragamanam vrataparipā lanamathvā dānam

Gyanviheenah sarvamatena muktim na bhajati jammashatena | Bhaja || 17 ||

इति श्रीशङ्कराचार्यविरचितं चर्पटपञ्जरिकास्तोत्रं सम्पूर्णम्।

कर क्योंकि मृत्यु के समीप आने पर 'डुकृञ्-करणे' की रटन रक्षा नहीं कर सकेगी || 7 ||

इस संसार में पुनः-पुनः जन्म, पुनः-पुनः मरण और बारम्बार माता के गर्भ में रहना पड़ता है! अतः हे मुरारे! मैं आपकी शरण हूँ, इस दुस्तर और अपार संसार से कृपया मुझे पार कीजिए! इस प्रकार! हे मूढ़! तू तो सदा गोविन्द का ही भजन कर, क्योंकि मृत्यु के समीप आने पर 'डुकृञ् करणे' की रटना रक्षा नहीं कर सकेगी || 8 ||

रात्रि-दिन, पक्ष, मास, अयन और वर्ष कितनी ही बार आए.... और गए तो भी लोग ईर्ष्या आशा को नहीं छोड़ते; अतः हे मूढ़! तू सदा गोविन्द का ही भजन कर क्योंकि मृत्यु के समीप आने पर यह 'डुकृञ करणे' की रटना रक्षा नहीं कर सकेगी॥ 9॥

अवस्था ढलने पर काम-विचार कैसा? जल सूखने पर जलाशय क्या? तथा धन नष्ट होने पर परिवार ही क्या? इसी प्रकार तत्त्व ज्ञान होने पर संसार ही कहाँ रह सकता है? अतः हे मूढ़! सदा गोविन्द को ही भज, क्योंकि मृत्यु समीप आने पर यह 'डुकृन्ज् करणे' की रटना रक्षा न कर सकेगी!॥ 10॥

नारी के स्तनों और नाभिनिवेश में मिथ्या माया और मोह का ही आवेश है, ये मांस और मेद ही के विकार हैं—ऐसा बार-बार मन में

[This completes Shankaracharya crcatred 'Char patpanjari ka Strotra']

-sorrows. Still people don't care to rid themselves of illusive hopes and petty jealousies. None is there to seek Brahman (Supreme Being). Hence worship Govinda, O fool! How will the rules of grammar help you when dcath is nigh || 7 ||

Repeated births and deaths in this world with innumerable times stay in the mother's womb ! O Enemy of Mura [ān epithet of Lord Vishnu or Lord Krishna] I seek shelter in your shadow. Kindly shed your grace upon me to make me cross this difficult and vast span of metempsycosis ||8||

Innumerable times have come and gone ; days, nights, fortnights, months, half years and years-but the people couldn't shed their illusive hopes and jealousy. Hence O fool ! Worship ever Govinda because how will the rules of grammar help when death is nigh || 9 ||

Of what use is sexual passion when age has withered ? Of what purpose is a pond when its water has dried up ? What is family when your wealth is destroyed ? Similarity, when enlightened by this rich knowledge of what significance is this whole world ? Hence, O fool, worship Govinda because how will the rulcs of grammar help you when your death is nigh ! || 10 ||

It is the illusions caused by infatuation that attracts one towards a woman's breasts or the nave-region- other wise they are, in reality, only lumps of flesh ! Hammer this thought

विचार कर; हे मूढ़ ! सदा गोविन्द का भजन कर क्योंकि मृत्यु के समीप आने पर यह 'डुकृन्ज् करणे' की रटना रक्षा नहीं कर सकेगी॥ 11 ॥

स्वप्रवत् मिथ्या संसार की आस्था छोड़ कर 'तू कौन है, मैं कौन हूँ, कहाँ से आया हूँ, मेरी माता कौन और मेरे पिता कौन हैं ?' इस प्रकार सबको असार समझ क्योंकि मृत्यु के निकट आने पर 'डुकृञ् करणे' की रटना रक्षा न कर सकेगी ? || 12 ||

गीता और विष्णु सहस्त्रनाम का नित्य पाठ करना चाहिए, चित्त को संतजनों की संगति में लगाना चाहिए और दीन जनों को धन दान करना चाहिए। और हे मूढ़ ! नित्य गोविन्द का ही भजन कर क्योंकि मृत्यु के निकट आने पर 'डुकृञ् करणे' यह रटना रक्षा न कर सकेगी || 13 ||

जब तक प्राण शरीर में हैं तब तक ही लोग घर में कुशल पूछते हैं, प्राण निकलने पर शरीर का पतन हुआ कि फिर उसकी स्त्री भी उससे भय मानती है ! अतः हे मूढ़ नित्य गोविन्द को ही भज, क्योंकि मृत्य निकट आने पर 'डुकृञ् करणे' की रटन रक्षा न कर सकेगी || 14 ||

पहले सुख से स्त्री संभोग किया जाता है किन्तु पीछे शरीर में रोग घर कर लेते हैं। यद्यपि संसार में मरना अवश्य है तथापि लोग पापाचरण को नहीं छोड़ते। अतः हे मूढ़ ! सदा गोविन्द का भजन कर क्योंकि मृत्यु निकट आने पर 'डुकृञ् करणे' की रटना रक्षा न कर सकेगी || 15 ||

गले में पड़ी चिचड़ों की कन्था (माला) बना ली, पुण्यापुण्य से निराला मार्ग अवलम्बन कर लिया 'न मैं हूँ न तू है और न यह संसार है

ever in your mind and always worship Govnida ! O fool ! How will the rulcs of grammar help your when death is nigh ! || 11 ||

"Who am I, who are you ? wherefrom have I come ? who is my mother or father ?" idle fancies are these all, unreal and without substance. Give up this world which is nothing but a dream, worship Govinda, O fool ! Hence will the rulcs of grammar help your when death is nigh ? || 12 ||

One should always chant the Thousand Names of Lord Vishnu, read the Gita and devote one's attention to seeking the company of the noble persons and in distributing alms to the poor. And O fool ! Ever worship Govinda for how will the rulcs of grammar help you when death is nigh ? || 13 ||

Till you have life in you your family members will look after you. The moment your life quits the body your own people will get frightened of your body-even your wife will try to get rid of it. Hence of fool ? worship only Govinda. How will the rules of grammar help you when death is nigh ? || 14 ||

First you enjoy sex with your wife but later on a variety of diseases possess your body. Although death is inevitable yet the puople don't shed their vile coruduct. Hcme O Fool ! worship Govinda for how will the rules of grmmar help you when death is nigh || 15 ||

Even when one joins pieces of rags to form a garland for himself, selects his path of life amidst

—(ऐसा भी जान लिया) फिर भी किसलिए शोक किया जाता है ? अत: हे मूढ़ ! सदा गोविन्द का ही भजन कर क्योंकि मृत्यु निकट आने पर 'डुकृञ् करणे' की रटन रक्षा न कर सकेगी || 16 ||

चाहे गंगा सागर को जाय, चाहे नाना व्रतोपवासों का पालन अथवा दान कर तथापि बिना ज्ञान के इन सबसे सौ जन्मों में भी मुक्ति नहीं हो सकती ; अत: हे मूढ़ ! सर्वदा गोविन्द का भजन कर क्योंकि मृत्यु के निकट आने पर 'डुकृञ् करणे' या धन! हा कुटुम्ब!! हा संसार!!!) की रटना रक्षा न कर सकेगी || 17 ||

meritorius and demeritorious acts; 'neither am I nor you are since this whole world is unreal'-(having realised thus) still one grives for material losses? For what? Hence o fool! Worship Govinda for there rules of grammar won't help you when your death is migh ? || 16 ||

Even thorugh one goes to the Ganga Sagar[1] and leads a pious life by observing all fasts and continence of every kind, unless one gets this knowledge (that this world is unreal and transitory) one can't get Salvation no matter one lives a hundred lives. Hence, O fool ! worship Govinda for there rules of grammar will not help when your death is migh. || 17 ||

1. The holy place where the Ganga joins the sea.

corruptions and demeritorious acts. Indeed, and now you are aware this whole world is unreal. (Having realised this) still one craves for material things? Ever wonder? Hence O fool! Worship Govinda, for these rules of grammar won't help you when your death is near? ||16||

Even though one goes to the Ganga Sagar[1] and leads a pious life by observing all rules and continence of every kind, unless one gets this knowledge (that this world is unreal and transitory) one can't get Salvation, no matter one lives a hundred lives. Hence, O fool! worship Govinda for these rules of grammar will not help when your death is nigh. ||17||

1. A holy place where the Ganga joins the Sea.